STUDENT ACTIVITY WO

Entrepreneurship

Owning Your Future

Eleventh Edition

Steve Mariotti

**Founder,
Network for Teaching Entrepreneurship**

With Tony Towle
Edited by Neelam Patel

Prentice Hall

Boston Columbus Indianapolis New York San Francisco Upper Saddle River

Amsterdam Cape Town Dubai London Madrid Milan Munich Paris Montreal Toronto

Delhi Mexico City Sao Paulo Sydney Hong Kong Seoul Singapore Taipei Tokyo

Editor in Chief: Vernon R. Anthony
Acquisitions Editor: Gary Bauer
Editorial Assistant: Megan Heintz
Director of Marketing: David Gesell
Campaign Marketing Manager: Leigh Ann Sims
School Marketing Manager: Laura Cutone
Senior Operations Supervisor: Pat Tonneman
Text and Cover Designer: Amy Rosen
Cover Art: Jose Luis Pelaez/Blend Images/Jupiter Images

Content Reviewer: Rupa Mohan
Full-Service Project Management: Gleason Group, Inc., Norwalk, CT
Composition: PDS Associates, Ocean Township, NJ
Printer/Binder: Bind-Rite Graphics
Cover Printer: Lehigh-Phoenix Color
Text Font: ITC Galliard Std

This book is dedicated to:
Raymond Chambers; Landon Hilliard; Elizabeth, Charles G., and David H. Koch; James Lyle; and the Honorable John C. Whitehead

Special dedication to:
Diana Davis Spencer, Art Samberg, Mary Myers Kauppila, and the late Bernard A. Goldhirsh

Entrepreneurship: Owning Your Future is the 11th edition of NFTE's textbook. The 10th edition was titled *How to Start & Operate a Small Business*. The Network for Teaching Entrepreneurship was previously named the National Foundation for Teaching Entrepreneurship.

10 9 8 7 6 5

Prentice Hall
is an imprint of

www.pearsonhighered.com

ISBN 10:   0-13-515000-0
ISBN 13:   978-0-13-515000-9

STUDY GUIDE
TABLE OF CONTENTS

BUSINESS PLAN PROJECT
TABLE OF CONTENTS

Study
Guide

Name _____ Class _____ Date _____

Before You Begin

Think about the following question:

Have you ever considered starting your own business?

Answer: ☐ **Yes** ☐ **No**

If **Yes**, what kind of business would you like to create?

_____

_____

_____

_____

If **No**, why haven't you considered starting your own business?

_____

_____

_____

_____

What would be the best thing about owning your own business? What would be the worst?

_____

_____

_____

_____

_____

_____

_____

Concepts Review

STUDY GUIDE 1.1

1. What is an entrepreneur?

_____

_____

2. How do employees and entrepreneurs differ? Which would you rather be?

_____

_____

_____

_____

_____

_____

3. Why are most businesses considered small?

_____

_____

_____

4. What are the rewards of being an entrepreneur?

_____

_____

_____

_____

5. What are some risks that entrepreneurs face?

_____

_____

_____

_____

6. How have entrepreneurs changed the world?

_____

_____

7. Name a famous entrepreneur from the 1800s and describe his/her contribution.

_____

_____

_____

_____

8. Name a famous entrepreneur from the early 1900s and describe his/her contribution.

_____

_____

_____

_____

_____

9. Name a famous entrepreneur from the mid- to late-1900s and describe his/her contribution.

_____

_____

_____

_____

_____

10. What are some of the things to which today's entrepreneurs need to pay attention?

_____

_____

11. Should an entrepreneur give up if the business fails? Briefly explain your answer.

_____

_____

Name _____ Class _____ Date _____

Crossword

Use the clues below to solve the puzzle, which contains many vocabulary terms from Section 1.1.

Across

2. Entrepreneur from the 1800s who invented the phonograph

4. Computer company launched by Stephen Wozniak and Steve Jobs

6. A big reward of entrepreneurship is being self-_____

8. Providing products, services, and jobs has a positive effect on this

9. A _____ entrepreneur starts successful businesses repeatedly

10. Another word for 3 DOWN

13. One of two partners who started a successful motorcycle company in 1903

14. Organization that makes money by providing products or services

Down

1. Business that adopts practices aimed at improving the environment (2 words)

3. Program that provides on-the-job training in a business setting

5. Entrepreneur Russell Simmons' record company (2 words)

7. Someone who creates and runs a business

11. When you are your own boss, you can make your own _____

12. Person who works in a business owned by someone else

Name _____ Class _____ Date _____

Check Yourself

In the sentences below, fill in the blanks with the correct answer.

1. A(n) _____ is someone who creates and runs his or her own business.

2. A small business is one that has fewer than _____ employees.

3. A program that provides on-the-job training is called a(n) _____ or a(n) _____.

4. Before starting your business weigh the _____ vs. the _____.

5. Entrepreneurs can affect the economy, the _____, and the world.

6. One of Edison's achievements that changed the world was the _____.

7. Maggie Lena Walker's philosophy that made her a success was "_____".

8. Businesses that protect or improve the environment are called _____.

9. Today, the _____ is a primary resource for businesses.

Circle whether each statement is true or false.

10. True   False   An employee works in a business owned by someone else.

11. True   False   Small firms employ 90% of the U.S. workforce.

12. True   False   More than half of all businesses started in the U.S. each year fail.

13. True   False   Making money is the major reward of being an entrepreneur.

14. True   False   All entrepreneurs want their businesses to become big.

15. True   False   Serial entrepreneurs have one business, but many locations.

16. True   False   Becoming an entrepreneur is best tried when one is young.

17. True   False   Anyone can become an entrepreneur.

18. True   False   Entrepreneurs need to pay attention to social trends to be successful.

Extend Your Knowledge

Use the Internet to research Whole Foods Market, a successful company begun by young entrepreneurs. Prepare a presentation for the class describing the ways in which this business shows it cares about the environment and the communities in which it operates. Make sure the presentation is the length specified by the instructor.

Name _____ Class _____ Date _____

STUDY GUIDE
Section 1.2

Characteristics of an Entrepreneur

Before You Begin

Think about the following question:

What kinds of abilities are needed to run a business?

List all the abilities you can think of that a person might need to run a business. Be specific.

_____

_____

_____

_____

_____

From your list above, choose the five abilities you believe a person *most* needs to run a business. Then, for each of the five abilities, briefly describe why an entrepreneur needs that ability to run a business.

Ability	Why Does an Entrepreneur Need that Ability?

Concepts Review

1. What are common traits of American business owners, according to the U.S. Census Bureau?

   _____

   _____

   _____

   _____

   _____

   _____

2. Why is it important to do a self-assessment before becoming an entrepreneur?

   _____

   _____

   _____

3. What is the difference between an aptitude and an attitude?

   _____

   _____

   _____

4. Why is a positive attitude important to being entrepreneurial?

   _____

   _____

   _____

5. What are some of the personal characteristics that an entrepreneur needs to possess?

   _____

   _____

   _____

   _____

STUDY GUIDE 1.2

6. Name some skills that an entrepreneur needs to possess.

_____

_____

_____

_____

7. List six areas on which a person should focus to build his or her entrepreneurial potential.

_____

_____

_____

_____

_____

_____

8. Why is it beneficial for employees to study entrepreneurship?

_____

_____

_____

_____

9. What are the possible benefits to employees of thinking like an entrepreneur?

_____

_____

_____

10. Why is it important to develop a vision for your life?

_____

_____

_____

_____

Name _____ Class _____ Date _____

Crossword

Use the clues below to solve the puzzle, which contains many vocabulary terms from Section 1.2.

Across

1. Personality trait that makes you sensitive to the thoughts and feelings of others
3. Having _____ skills means you can listen well, write well, and speak well
6. Personality trait that gives you the desire to learn and ask questions
10. Natural ability to do a particular type of work or activity well
11. Personality trait that means you are truthful and sincere with others
12. Experienced person who provides guidance and shares knowledge
13. Ability that is learned through training and practice
14. Picture of what you want the future to be

Down

2. Having _____ skills means you know how to persuade, motivate, and lead others
4. Self-_____ is evaluating your strengths and weaknesses
5. Practice that gives employees opportunities to be creative and try out new ideas
7. Way of thinking about something that affects how you feel about it
8. Personality trait that enables you to take risks in spite of possible losses
9. Personality trait that gives you the ability to stay focused and meet deadlines

Check Yourself

In the sentences below, fill in the blanks with the correct answer.

1. The U.S. Census Bureau reports that _____ of business owners had some college education when they started the business.

2. A(n) _____ is an evaluation of your strengths and weaknesses.

3. Entrepreneurs typically have _____ attitudes.

4. Courage is a willingness to take _____ in spite of possible _____.

5. A skill is learned through _____ and _____.

6. An entrepreneur that listens carefully to people and also speaks and writes well has good _____.

7. Thinking like a(n) _____ helps a person be a better employee.

8. Volunteering in the community is one of the six ways to increase one's entrepreneurial _____.

Circle whether each statement is true or false.

9. True   False   An attitude is a natural ability to do well at a task or activity.

10. True   False   Enthusiatic entrepreneurs can see problems as opportunities.

11. True   False   Creativity is a characteristic needed to be a successful entrepreneur.

12. True   False   "People skills" help entrepreneurs analyze financial statements

13. True   False   Business knowledge can increase your entrepreneurial potential.

14. True   False   Most entrepreneurs work less than 40 hours per week.

15. True   False   People, both young and old, can become entrepreneurs.

16. True   False   Only entrepreneurs, not employees, need to study entrepreneurship.

Extend Your Knowledge

Write a two-page biography of a famous entrepreneur or business owner that focuses on his or her personal characteristics and skills. Describe how these traits helped this individual become successful in the business world.

STUDY GUIDE
Section 2.1

Importance of Entrepreneurship in the Economy

Before You Begin

Think about the following question:

Is making a profit a good thing?

Answer: ☐ **Yes**   ☐ **No**

If **Yes**, why is making a profit a good thing?

_____

_____

_____

_____

_____

If **No**, why is making a profit a bad thing?

_____

_____

_____

_____

_____

If **Yes**, is it okay for business owners and entrepreneurs to make really big profits? Why or why not?

_____

_____

_____

_____

_____

_____

Concepts Review

1. What is an economic system?

   _____

   _____

   _____

2. List the four fundamental questions of economics.

   _____

   _____

   _____

   _____

3. Name the three types of economic systems and briefly describe each one.

   _____

   _____

   _____

   _____

   _____

   _____

   _____

   _____

4. What is a supply and demand curve?

   _____

   _____

   _____

5. How is price affected by supply and demand?

   _____

   _____

   _____

6. What results from competition between suppliers in a market economy?

_____

_____

_____

_____

7. What results from competition between consumers in a market economy?

_____

_____

_____

_____

8. Why is profit motive important to entrepreneurs?

_____

_____

_____

_____

9. What is the "economics of one unit"?

_____

_____

_____

_____

10. How does a non-profit organization differ from a for-profit business?

_____

_____

_____

_____

Crossword

Use the clues below to solve the puzzle, which contains many vocabulary terms from Section 2.1.

Across

1. Quantity of goods and services consumers are willing to buy at a specific price and time

7. Government controls the production, allocation, and price of goods and services in a _____ economy

8. Transaction in which both suppliers and consumers believe they benefit (2 words)

12. On a graph, this shows the quantity and price relationship acceptable to suppliers (2 words)

13. On a graph, the _____ point is where supply and demand are balanced

14. Suppliers and consumers control the production, allocation, and price of goods and services in a _____ economy

Down

2. Profit _____ encourages an entrepreneur to accept the risks of starting a new business

3. In a _____ organization, money comes in part from grants and donations

4. On a graph, this shows the quantity and price relationship acceptable to consumers (2 words)

5. Cash and goods that a business owns

6. Social science concerned with the flow of goods and services between people

9. In a free _____ system, people are free to own and operate a business

10. Quantity of goods and services a business is willing to sell at a specific price and time

11. Shortage of goods and services to meet the demand results in this

Check Yourself

In the sentences below, fill in the blanks with the correct answer.

1. An economic system is used by society to allocate _____ for its people and to cope with _____.

2. The equilibrium point is the point on a supply and demand curve where supply and demand are _____.

3. An important aspect of a market economy is _____ exchange.

4. The _____ economic system is also called capitalism or free enterprise.

5. Competition between entrepreneurs selling the same goods or services pushes prices _____.

6. Entrepreneurs make a profit when the amount of money coming into a business is _____ than the business's expenses.

7. A nonprofit organization operates solely to serve the good of _____.

Circle whether each statement is true or false.

8. True   False   The command system is the best economic system for entrepreneurs.

9. True   False   People play the central role in an economy.

10. True   False   Consumers buy more of a product when its price is low.

11. True   False   The supply and demand curve is a tool used by entrepreneurs.

12. True   False   Suppliers often charge higher prices when demand is low.

13. True   False   The profit motive encourages entrepreneurs to start businesses.

14. True   False   Earning a profit is the only reason that people start businesses.

15. True   False   Non-profit organizations are not allowed to make a profit.

Extend Your Knowledge

Hybrid cars are considered environmentally friendly, because they use less gasoline than traditional cars. Prepare a PowerPoint slide show for the class that describes the current supply and demand relationship for hybrid cars. List and explain factors that could cause supply to increase or decrease in the future. Also list and explain factors that could cause demand to increase or decrease in the future. Make sure the slide show is the length specified by the instructor.

STUDY GUIDE
Section 2.2

Thinking Globally, Acting Locally

Before You Begin

Think about the following question:

Do you care if the clothes you buy are made in America?

Answer: ☐ **Yes** ☐ **No**

If **Yes**, explain why it is important to you to buy American-made clothing.

_____

_____

_____

_____

_____

If **No**, describe why this is not a factor in your clothes-buying choices.

_____

_____

_____

_____

_____

Which countries do you believe supply most of the clothing sold in America?

_____

_____

_____

_____

_____

Concepts Review

1. What is the global economy?

   _____

   _____

   _____

2. How does scarcity affect global trade?

   _____

   _____

   _____

3. What is the difference between importing and exporting?

   _____

   _____

   _____

   _____

4. Name some ways in which entrepreneurs can benefit from international trade.

   _____

   _____

   _____

   _____

   _____

5. Why are tariffs and quotas considered trade barriers?

   _____

   _____

   _____

   _____

STUDY GUIDE 2.2

6. How can U.S. entrepreneurs participate in fair trade?

_____

_____

_____

7. From a business standpoint, why should entrepreneurs respect the cultures of their foreign trading partners?

_____

_____

_____

_____

8. What do entrepreneurs need to know about foreign exchange rates?

_____

_____

_____

9. Name some ways in which entrepreneurs can benefit their local economies.

_____

_____

_____

_____

_____

_____

10. Why is sustainable economic development an important goal?

_____

_____

_____

_____

Name _____ Class _____ Date _____

Crossword

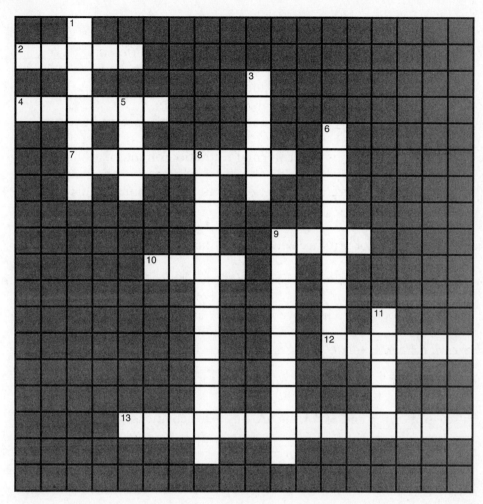

Use the clues below to solve the puzzle, which contains many vocabulary terms from Section 2.2.

Across

2. With 1 DOWN, governmental restriction on international exchange of goods and services

4. Fee that importers must pay on the goods they import

7. Social rules and customs practiced by a particular culture

9. Currency unit of the European Union

10. Currency unit of China

12. _____ economy is the flow of goods and services around the world

13. Development that does not harm but maintains natural resources for future generations

Down

1. With 2 ACROSS, governmental restriction on international exchange of goods and services

3. Limit on the quantity of a product that can be imported into a country

5. _____ trade ensures that small producers earn sufficient profit on their goods

6. Bringing goods and services into a country from foreign suppliers

8. Foreign _____ is the value of one currency unit in relation to another (2 words)

9. Sending goods and services from one country to foreign consumers

11. _____ economy covers a limited area, such as a town

STUDY GUIDE 2.2

Check Yourself

In the sentences below, fill in the blanks with the correct answer.

1. The global economy involves trading between people from different _____.

2. A country that _____ products buys them from foreign sellers.

3. A country that _____ products sells them to foreign buyers.

4. A trade _____ is governmental restriction on international trade.

5. The value of a country's currency in relation to another country's currency is the _____.

6. The goal of fair trade is for producers in poor nations to earn sufficient _____.

7. Entrepreneurs can benefit their local economies by hiring _____ employees.

8. The goal of sustainability is to improve human life and the _____.

Circle whether each statement is true or false.

9. True   False   Global trade provides opportunities for entrepreneurs.

10. True   False   Importing and exporting are business activities.

11. True   False   Services can not be exported.

12. True   False   The Internet makes it easier to participate in international trade.

13. True   False   Cultural customs are the same in every country around the world.

14. True   False   Fair trade helps entrepreneurs in developing countries.

15. True   False   Trade barriers make it easier for entrepreneurs to import and export.

16. True   False   Sustainable economic development is bad for the global economy.

Extend Your Knowledge

Make a poster that lists the foreign exchange rates for the U.S. dollar in five other countries. Also, list five products that an American entrepreneur might wish to sell over the Internet to consumers in these countries. Determine (or estimate) a price in U.S. dollars for each product. Use the foreign exchange rates to calculate the price of each product in the five respective foreign currencies. Show all of these prices on the poster. Also, give the teacher a piece of paper showing the mathematical calculations you used to determine the prices in the foreign currencies.

Name _____ Class _____ Date _____

Before You Begin

Think about the following question:

When I think of "business," what type of business do I think of first?

_____

What is a good definition of "business"?

_____

_____

_____

_____

_____

Name some categories that could be used to describe businesses (for example, large or small).

_____

_____

_____

_____

_____

Do you think most businesses sell their goods or services to other businesses or to the general public? Explain.

_____

_____

_____

_____

_____

_____

Concepts Review

1. Who are the primary customers of manufacturing businesses? Why?

_____

_____

_____

_____

_____

2. Who are the primary customers of wholesaling businesses? Why?

_____

_____

_____

_____

_____

3. Who are the primary customers of retailing businesses? Why?

_____

_____

_____

_____

_____

4. What does a service business do?

_____

_____

5. Name some services that service businesses provide.

_____

_____

_____

_____

Name _____ Class_____ Date _____

6. List some special types of businesses that combine aspects of the other four business types.

_____

_____

_____

7. Which business type was most common in America in the 1950s?

_____

_____

_____

8. What is a franchise?

_____

_____

_____

_____

_____

9. Which business type became most common in America in the 2000s?

_____

_____

_____

10. What are NAICS codes?

_____

_____

_____

11. Which business type is expected to dominate the U.S. economy in the future?

_____

_____

_____

Crossword

Use the clues below to solve the puzzle, which contains many vocabulary terms from Section 3.1.

Across

3. Popular fast-food example of 6 ACROSS

4. Mining is an example of this type of business

6. Arrangement in which an established business sells the right to set up the business in another location

9. Type of goods sold directly to the public

11. A dry cleaner or auto-repair shop is an example of this type of business

12. Abbreviation for system that assigns a numeric code to North American industries based on their primary function

13. Publication used by retailers to sell their goods and services

14. Nontraditional location for retail stores

Down

1. Businesses need a reseller's _____ to purchase goods tax-free from wholesalers

2. A grocery store or boutique is an example of this type of business

3. Type of business that converts materials into goods that can be sold by others

5. Consulting service that is one of the fastest-growing industries

7. Type of goods that include metal and plastic parts

8. Type of business that buys goods in large quantities for resale to retailers

10. Type of business that involves the sale of agricultural products

Check Yourself

In the sentences below, fill in the blanks with the correct answer.

1. The two typical types of manufactured goods are _____ and _____.

2. Wholesalers provide a link between _____ businesses and _____ businesses.

3. Stores, shops, and boutiques are examples of _____ businesses.

4. Wholesaling and retailing businesses are also known as _____ businesses.

5. Babysitting and music lessons are examples of _____ businesses.

6. In many states retailers must have a _____ permit to purchase goods tax-free from wholesalers and collect sales tax from the end buyers.

7. Between the 1950s and the 2000s _____ businesses became much less dominant and _____ businesses became much more dominant.

8. A _____ is a business that purchases the right to use an established company's name and operating plan to sell products or services.

Circle whether each statement is true or false.

9. True   False   Most wholesalers sell directly to the public.

10. True   False   A retailer might sell products from a store or over the Internet.

11. True   False   Large manufacturing companies typically sell products to wholesalers.

12. True   False   Retailers resell products purchased from wholesaling businesses.

13. True   False   Most service businesses are also manufacturers.

14. True   False   Manufacturing is the dominant business type in America today.

15. True   False   Most business start-ups in recent years have been service businesses.

16. True   False   McDonald's restaurants are manufacturing businesses.

Extend Your Knowledge

The business magazine *Entrepreneur* publishes an annual list called the "Hot 100." These are the one hundred fastest-growing small businesses in the United States. Research the latest list and prepare a presentation for the class about it. Include a table or graph in which you categorize the 100 companies by the business types covered in this section. Make sure your presentation is the length specified by the instructor.

Name _____ Class _____ Date _____

STUDY GUIDE 3.2

Types of Business Ownership

Before You Begin

Think about the following question:

If a business fails, should the owner be responsible for paying its debts, even if it means selling a home or car?

Answer: ☐ **Yes** ☐ **No**

If **Yes**, explain why you believe a business owner should be personally responsible for the debts of his or her business.

_____

_____

_____

_____

_____

If **No**, explain why you believe a business owner should not be personally responsible for the debts of his or her business.

_____

_____

_____

_____

_____

Whose fault is it if a business fails? Explain.

_____

_____

_____

_____

_____

_____

Concepts Review

1. What is liability?

   _____

   _____

2. What is the difference between limited liability and unlimited liability?

   _____

   _____

   _____

3. What are some of the advantages and disadvantages of forming a sole proprietorship?

   _____

   _____

   _____

   _____

   _____

4. What are some of the advantages and disadvantages of forming a partnership?

   _____

   _____

   _____

   _____

   _____

   _____

5. What is the difference between a general partnership and a limited partnership?

   _____

   _____

   _____

   _____

STUDY GUIDE 3.2

STUDY GUIDE 3.2

6. What are some of the advantages and disadvantages of forming a corporation?

_____

_____

_____

_____

_____

_____

_____

7. How does a C corporation differ from a subchapter S corporation?

_____

_____

_____

8. Why has the limited liability company become a popular business ownership option?

_____

_____

_____

9. How is a nonprofit corporation different from a for-profit corporation?

_____

_____

_____

_____

_____

10. What is a cooperative?

_____

_____

_____

Crossword

Use the clues below to solve the puzzle, which contains many vocabulary terms from Section 3.2.

Across

1. Owner of a corporation

5. Portion of profit that owners of 8 ACROSS may earn

8. Unit of ownership in a corporation is a _____ of stock

10. With 14 DOWN, type of business in which the owner personally bears all legal and financial responsibility

11. Two or more individuals legally share this type of business

12. In this type of 9 DOWN, the owner cannot be legally forced to pay a business's debts

13. What D.B.A. stands for

15. In this type of 9 DOWN, the owner can be legally forced to pay a business's debts

Down

2. The business itself is legally a type of "person" in this type of ownership

3. To set up a 2 DOWN so it can be regulated by the laws of its state

4. Corporate decision-making is made by a board of _____

6. Unlike a C corporation, a _____ S corporation is not taxed twice

7. Business owned and operated for the benefit of its members

9. Legal responsibility of a business owner to use personal assets to pay the debts of the business

14. With 10 ACROSS, type of business in which the owner personally bears all legal and financial responsibility

Check Yourself

In the sentences below, fill in the blanks with the correct answer.

1. A business owner with _____ liability might have to pay off business debts using his or her personal money and possessions.

2. Liability is a _____ obligation.

3. The _____ is the simplest option for business ownership.

4. Partners share the management, profits, and liability of their business based on the terms of their _____.

5. Shareholders or stockholders are the owners of a _____.

6. To _____ means to set up a corporation in accordance with the laws of the state in which the business is located.

7. A cooperative is a business owned by its _____.

Circle whether each statement is true or false.

8. True   False   Entrepreneurs with limited liability put their personal assets at risk.

9. True   False   The level of liability depends on the type of business ownership.

10. True   False   A sole proprietorship provides limited liability to the business owner.

11. True   False   In a general partnership all partners have unlimited liability.

12. True   False   A corporation is easier to set up than a sole proprietorship.

13. True   False   C corporations and S corporations differ in how they are taxed.

14. True   False   Farmers often form cooperatives to buy farming equipment.

15. True   False   A limited liability company is owned by its stockholders.

Extend Your Knowledge

Use Internet resources to learn about incorporating a business in your state. Write an instructional "how-to" booklet, or paper, in which you describe the steps and fees required to incorporate. Make sure your booklet or paper is the length specified by the instructor.

STUDY GUIDE
Section 4.1

Communicating in Business

Before You Begin

Think about the following question:

Is it dishonest to change the way you communicate in business compared to your everyday method?

Answer: ☐ **Yes** ☐ **No**

If **Yes**, why is it dishonest?

_____

_____

_____

Is it dishonest to use different ways of communicating when talking to your friends than when talking to your parents or teachers? Explain.

_____

_____

_____

_____

Should you change your communication style depending on your audience? Why or why not?

_____

_____

_____

_____

If your communication style caused you to lose business, would you change it? Why or why not?

_____

_____

_____

_____

STUDY GUIDE 4.1

Concepts Review

1. What are the six qualities of effective business communication?

_____

_____

_____

2. What kinds of tone are inappropriate for business communications?

_____

_____

3. What are the four types of written business communication?

_____

_____

4. Why should written communications be reread and proofread before being sent out?

_____

_____

_____

_____

_____

_____

5. What is the difference between a business letter and a memo?

_____

_____

_____

_____

_____

_____

Name _____ Class _____ Date _____

6. What are the advantages and disadvantages of using e-mail for business communications?

_____

_____

_____

_____

_____

_____

7. What elements should be included in a fax cover sheet?

_____

_____

_____

8. What are five suggestions for being a good speaker?

_____

_____

_____

9. How do a telephone call, a conference call, and a videoconference differ from one another?

_____

_____

_____

10. How does instant messaging combine aspects of writing and speaking?

_____

_____

11. How is active listening a two-part process.

_____

_____

Crossword

Use the clues below to solve the puzzle, which contains many vocabulary terms from Section 4.1.

Across

1. With 15 DOWN, what "cc:" in a letter stands for

3. With 4 DOWN, what "IM" stands for

6. Greeting that starts a letter

8. In good business communication, it's important to keep it short and _____

10. People in different locations can speak to each other during a conference _____

12. Symbol used in texting that expresses emotion, such as :-)

14. Meeting that allows participants in different locations to see and hear each other through monitors and speakers

Down

2. Identifying information (name, phone number) added automatically to the end of an e-mail message

4. With 3 ACROSS, what "IM" stands for

5. What "fax" is short for

7. Note written to people within a business

9. _____ listening means focusing on the speaker and giving feedback

11. Camera attached to a computer during a Web conference

13. Replying to an e-mail creates a message _____ that shows previous messages

15. With 1 ACROSS, what "cc:" in a letter stands for

Name _____ Class _____ Date _____

Check Yourself

In the sentences below, fill in the blanks with the correct answer.

1. The communications rule KISS stands for "keep it _____ and _____."

2. Written communications create a _____ trail that helps back up your claims.

3. To draw in the entire audience when you speak, be sure to look and nod at each _____.

4. In written communications the abbreviation cc stands for _____.

5. The closing to a business letter includes your _____ in print and your signature.

6. Instant messaging is also known as _____.

7. The purpose of _____ is to let the speaker know you understand what is being said.

8. For communication to be relevant you must supply the right _____ to the right _____.

Circle whether each statement is true or false.

9. True   False   Different types of communication are required for different situations.

10. True   False   Some messages are best put in writing for legal reasons.

11. True   False   Business letters are best for shorter and less official messages.

12. True   False   On a business telephone call you should identify yourself right away.

13. True   False   Memos are brief notes sent to people outside the business.

14. True   False   Sensitive business information is best transmitted by e-mail.

15. True   False   Instant messaging provides good privacy for business messages.

16. True   False   The purpose of active listening is to improve communication.

Extend Your Knowledge

Netiquette is a combination of the words Internet and etiquette (appropriate social conduct). Thus, business netiquette refers to conducting online communications in an appropriate manner. Use Internet resources, such as business journals, to research guidelines for proper business netiquette. Present your findings to the class in a short presentation. Make sure it is the length specified by the instructor.

STUDY GUIDE 4.2

STUDY GUIDE
Section 4.2

Negotiating

Before You Begin

Think about the following question:

When negotiating, should someone win?

Answer: ☐ **Yes**   ☐ **No**

Do you agree that negotiation is about compromise not winning? Write a short essay expressing your opinion and share it with the class.

_____

_____

_____

_____

_____

_____

_____

_____

_____

_____

_____

_____

_____

_____

_____

_____

_____

Concepts Review

1. What must each party be willing to do for a negotiation to succeed?

_____

_____

_____

_____

2. List the four questions you should ask yourself when preparing to negotiate.

_____

_____

_____

_____

_____

3. What are the seven guidelines for productive negotiating?

_____

_____

_____

_____

4. How are concessions related to wants and needs?

_____

_____

_____

_____

5. What should take place after an agreement is reached through negotiation?

_____

_____

_____

6. What should you do if you cannot meet the commitments you made in the negotiation agreement?

_____

_____

_____

_____

7. What should you do if the other party cannot meet the commitments he or she made in the negotiation agreement?

_____

_____

_____

8. Why are values important in business negotiations?

_____

_____

_____

_____

9. Name some aspects of social etiquette that are important in international business negotiations.

_____

_____

_____

_____

10. Name some aspects of negotiation etiquette that are important in international business negotiations.

_____

_____

_____

_____

Crossword

Use the clues below to solve the puzzle, which contains many vocabulary terms from Section 4.2.

Across

2. Process in which people use communication to reach an agreement or solve a problem

5. Agreement arrived at when everyone gives up something but gets something in return

6. Type of nonverbal language that can show if one is open to discussion

8. The role of this in public life can affect business negotiations

9. What you're willing to give up when working to reach an agreement

12. Beliefs you have about your future

13. Quality or way of doing something that you believe is important and worthwhile

Down

1. A negotiation can have short-term and long-term _____

3. In a negotiation, parties should look for common _____ to agree on

4. _____ negotiations involve people from different countries

7. _____ in good faith means parties resolve their differences to come to an agreement

10. In a negotiation, you should focus on what you _____

11. Type of etiquette that considers customs, such as how to greet someone

Name _____ Class _____ Date _____

Check Yourself

In the sentences below, fill in the blanks with the correct answer.

1. Negotiation is important to business because it helps people achieve a shared goal of making the _____.

2. In a business negotiation, focus on meeting your needs before meeting your _____.

3. For a negotiation to be fair to all parties, the trade-offs should be roughly _____.

4. Part of negotiating in good faith is acting in accordance with your _____.

5. The purpose of learning and practicing foreign etiquette is to show _____ for the culture of the other parties in an international negotiation.

6. Negotiation requires give and _____ by each party.

7. Negotiation involves solving problems in a way that is acceptable to _____.

8. Concessions should be wants rather than _____.

Circle whether each statement is true or false.

9. True   False   Failed negotiations are bad for business and can be bad for the economy.

10. True   False   Concessions are sacrifices that negotiating parties are willing to make.

11. True   False   A need is something that is essential to your business's survival.

12. True   False   Offers made during negotiations should be oral rather than written.

13. True   False   Making concessions leads to a compromise during a negotiation.

14. True   False   Communication ends between the parties after the agreement is final.

15. True   False   Your values reflect your deeply held beliefs.

16. True   False   A cultural preference is either right or wrong.

Extend Your Knowledge

Imagine that a large company wants to negotiate with you about buying your successful small business, which has two locations and employs more than 20 people. Use the Internet to research common negotiating points for companies involved in purchasing or merging with each other. Now, write your negotiating plan. Include all the points you want to cover during the negotiations and any concessions you are willing to make.

STUDY GUIDE
Section 5.1

Ethical Business Behavior

Before You Begin

Think about the following question:

One rule everyone should live by is …

_____

List all the values you can think of that everyone should hold.

_____

_____

_____

_____

_____

From your list above, choose the one value you believe is most important. Why is it most important?

_____

_____

_____

_____

_____

Name five specific actions or behaviors that you believe would show what a person's most important value is.

_____

_____

_____

_____

_____

Concepts Review

1. What does it mean to act ethically?

_____

_____

_____

2. How are values and ethics related to culture?

_____

_____

_____

_____

3. List three practical reasons why a business should behave ethically.

_____

_____

_____

_____

_____

_____

4. List three ways to foster an ethical atmosphere in the workplace.

_____

_____

_____

5. How can a business create transparency?

_____

_____

_____

_____

6. What are three positive outcomes that a code of ethics can bring to your busness?

_____

_____

_____

_____

7. Name some types of intellectual property.

_____

_____

8. What is the difference between a copyright and a patent?

_____

_____

_____

9. Which two symbols are associated with trademarks and what do they mean?

_____

_____

_____

_____

_____

10. Give two examples of entrepreneurs behaving unethically through infringing on the copyrights of intellectual property.

_____

_____

_____

_____

11. What is a conflict of interest?

_____

_____

Crossword

Use the clues below to solve the puzzle, which contains many vocabulary terms from Section 5.1.

Across

3. With 5 ACROSS, term for someone who reports illegal or unethical conduct

5. With 3 ACROSS, term for someone who reports illegal or unethical conduct

7. Music and inventions are examples of _____ property

9. Violation of a patent-holder's rights

11. Exclusive right to perform, display, copy, or distribute an artistic work

13. Friendship and helping others are examples of _____ values

14. Openness and accountability in business decisions and actions

Down

1. Interactive electronic forms of communication (2 words)

2. _____ of interest exists when personal considerations and professional obligations interfere with each other

4. With 12 DOWN, status of an invention whose patent has expired

6. Symbol that indicates a brand is protected and cannot be used by another business

8. Exclusive right to make, use, or sell a device or process

10. Set of moral principles that govern decisions and actions

12. With 4 DOWN, status of an invention whose patent has expired

Name _____Class_____Date _____

Check Yourself

In the sentences below, fill in the blanks with the correct answer.

1. Ethics are a set of _____ principles that govern decisions and actions.

2. The golden rule is "do unto others as you would have them do unto _____."

3. A business creates transparency by _____ with people inside and outside the company about its decisions and actions.

4. The expression "the buck stops here" means that an individual or business takes _____ for decisions.

5. A code of ethics describes a company's moral philosophy and gives _____ guidelines for carrying it out.

6. An industrial design, product, or process is intellectual property protected by a _____.

7. Copyrights protect _____ expressions, such as musical compositions or literary works.

Circle whether each statement is true or false.

8. True   False   All cultures express and enforce ethical standards in the same way.

9. True   False   People trust a company that has a reputation for acting ethically.

10. True   False   Transparency lets people see what a business is doing, and why.

11. True   False   Everyone has a right to know everything a company does.

12. True   False   Ethical businesses discourage and punish whistle-blowers.

13. True   False   People can have the same values but act upon them differently.

14. True   False   Patents protect music and paintings from being copied.

Extend Your Knowledge

Businesses can get into legal trouble when they use another company's intellectual property without permission. Use the Internet to research the case of Ty, Inc. (maker of Beanie Babies) against Softbelly's, Inc. Describe the case to the class. What happened and what was the outcome? Also discuss how this case serves as a lesson to new entrepreneurs who may be tempted to copy too closely the products of successful companies. Make sure your talk is the length specified by the instructor.

Name _____ Class _____ Date _____

STUDY GUIDE 5.2

Socially Responsible Business & Philanthropy

Before You Begin

Think about the following question:

What three things would make the world a better place?

List three things that would make the world a better place. Be specific.

1. _____

2. _____

3. _____

If your business made a net profit of $10,000 this year, to which charities would you donate $100 or more. (To see the many charities that exist in the United States, check out The Foundation Center at http://fdncenter.org.) Explain how your contribution would make the world a better place.

_____

_____

_____

_____

_____

_____

_____

_____

_____

_____

_____

_____

_____

Concepts Review

1. What is corporate social responsibility?

   _____

   _____

2. List the responsibilities that businesses have to their employees.

   _____

   _____

   _____

   _____

3. What four qualities should businesses put into practice to have a responsible relationship with their customers?

   _____

   _____

4. Give some examples of how businesses act responsibly toward their suppliers.

   _____

   _____

   _____

   _____

   _____

   _____

5. How should entrepreneurs treat their business's investors and creditors?

   _____

   _____

   _____

   _____

   _____

6. If you could create your own foundation, what would it do? Whom would it help? What name would you give it? Write a short mission statement for your foundation.

_____

_____

_____

_____

_____

_____

_____

_____

7. What is a social issue that you think is important? Find at least five nonprofit organizations that address this issue. Conduct research on each. What are their mission statements? How do they make a difference through their work?

_____

_____

_____

_____

_____

_____

_____

_____

_____

_____

_____

8. What are two positive outcomes of cause-related marketing?

_____

_____

Crossword

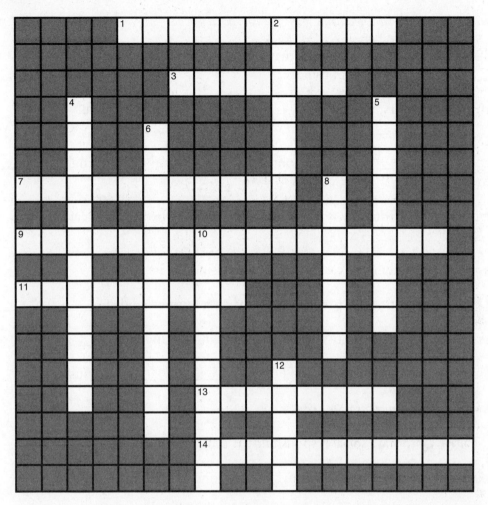

Use the clues below to solve the puzzle, which contains many vocabulary terms from Section 5.2.

Across

1. Financial support of an event or service in exchange for advertising

3. With 13 ACROSS, buying from suppliers who respect workers' rights

7. Type of design that preserves resources for future generations

9. Donation in which a business contributes a percentage of the sale price to a charity (2 words)

11. To do charitable work without pay

13. With 3 ACROSS, buying from suppliers who respect workers' rights

14. Solar power and wind are examples of _____ energy

Down

2. What a business can do with paper and plastic to save money and help the environment

4. Type of marketing that is a beneficial partnership between a business and a nonprofit group (2 words)

5. A carbon _____ is the amount of carbon you use and release into the environment

6. Donating money and other resources for socially beneficial causes

8. Type of food product made without manufactured chemicals

10. Efficient, money-saving appliances have this label (2 words)

12. To an environmentalist, this color means protecting natural resources

Check Yourself

In the sentences below, fill in the blanks with the correct answer.

1. "Doing well by doing good" means that corporate social responsibility can result in _____ for a business.

2. An entrepreneur's first responsibility is to himself or herself and to all the _____ that rely on the business.

3. Attracting _____ customers costs more than maintaining _____ customers.

4. Doing business electronically is environmentally friendly because it means using less _____.

5. A measure of the amount of carbon used by a business is its carbon _____.

6. Cause-related marketing is a partnership between a business and a _____.

7. Businesses sponsor community events or services in exchange for _____.

8. An in-kind donation is a gift of a good or _____ by a business.

Circle whether each statement is true or false.

9. True   False   Corporate social responsibility is only practiced by large companies.

10. True   False   The word "philanthropy" means "one who loves humankind."

11. True   False   Sustainable design considers the long-term impacts of a product.

12. True   False   Entrepreneurs should use competing suppliers as bargaining chips to lower prices.

13. True   False   Entrepreneurs should show respect to their investors and creditors.

14. True   False   Fair-trade sales have fallen in the last decade.

15. True   False   Recycling helps a business be more energy-efficient.

16. True   False   Greenwashing is an ethical practice.

Extend Your Knowledge

Write a biography about a famous philanthropist who has generously donated to socially beneficial causes. How did this person become successful at business? What causes did (or does) he or she support? Why? How has this person helped make the world a better place? Make sure your paper is the length specified by the instructor.

Name _____ Class _____ Date _____

What Is a Business Plan?

Before You Begin

Think about the following question:

If I were going to do something important, would I plan before I did it?

Answer: ☐ Yes ☐ No

If **Yes**, why would you plan first?

_____

_____

_____

_____

_____

_____

If **No**, why wouldn't you plan?

_____

_____

_____

_____

_____

_____

What is a plan and what is its purpose?

_____

_____

_____

_____

_____

_____

Concepts Review

1. What does the process of writing a business plan force an entrepreneur to do?

_____

_____

_____

2. How does a well-written business plan benefit an entrepreneur?

_____

_____

_____

_____

_____

_____

_____

3. What two factors determine which type of business plan should be prepared?

_____

_____

_____

4. What are the four main types of business plans?

_____

_____

_____

5. What are the "Three C's" that should be addressed in a business plan?

_____

_____

6. List the seven parts of an investor's business plan.

_____

_____

_____

_____

7. What elements are included in the "Business Idea" section of a written business plan?

_____

_____

_____

_____

8. What are the eight elements that should be included in the executive summary of a business plan?

_____

_____

_____

_____

_____

_____

9. Name two Internet resources for information about business plans.

_____

_____

10. What two questions should an entrepreneur consider early in the process of developing a business plan?

_____

_____

_____

_____

Crossword

Use the clues below to solve the puzzle, which contains many vocabulary terms from Section 6.1.

Across

1. With 12 ACROSS, a business plan's list of highlights and key selling points

6. A business plan must discuss the type of _____, such as partnership or corporation

7. Business plan section that provides cash flow data

9. With 11 DOWN, a 30-second explanation of an idea for a new business

10. One of the Three C's for a business plan

12. With 1 ACROSS, a business plan's list of highlights and key selling points

13. With 14 ACROSS, type of business plan given as a slide show with a running narrative

14. With 13 ACROSS, type of business plan given as a slide show with a running narrative

Down

2. Part of a business plan that describes the size of your target audience and your competition (2 words)

3. One of the Three C's for a business plan

4. One of the Three C's for a business plan

5. Audience for a detailed business plan

8. A business plan idea is typically for a product or _____

11. With 9 ACROSS, a 30-second explanation of an idea for a new business

Check Yourself

In the sentences below, fill in the blanks with the correct answer.

1. A business plan for a for-profit business typically focuses on the entrepreneur's _____ goals.

2. One example of a quick-summary type of business plan is called an _____ pitch.

3. The oral-presentation type of business plan includes a colorful _____.

4. The purpose of the oral presentation is to interest potential _____ in reading the detailed business plan.

5. A quick-summary type of business plan lasts no more than _____ minutes.

6. A written business plan should be no more than _____ typed pages.

7. The executive summary of a written business plan should be _____ pages or less.

8. It is better to discover that a business won't work on _____ before you invest significant time and money.

Circle whether each statement is true or false.

9. True   False   A well-written business plan never needs to be revised.

10. True   False   The quick-summary type of business plan is a written plan.

11. True   False   An operational business plan is for use within the business only.

12. True   False   Potential investors will reject a poorly written business plan.

13. True   False   A well-written business plan should take at least three hours to read.

14. True   False   Developing a business plan is not a simple, straightforward process.

15. True   False   A business plan describes the goals of the business.

16. True   False   An investor's business plan is a brief synopsis of the business idea.

Extend Your Knowledge

Check out the Websites of the Small Business Administration (www.sba.gov) and www.entrepreneur.com for tips for entrepreneurs on creating business plans for new businesses. Write a short report detailing your findings. Make sure the report is the length specified by the instructor.

STUDY GUIDE
Section 6.2

What Is a Business Opportunity?

Before You Begin

Think about the following question:

If you started a business, what would it be?

_____

Why do you believe there would be demand from customers for this business?

_____

_____

_____

_____

_____

What skills and resources do you have that could make this business successful?

_____

_____

_____

_____

_____

What should you do to determine if this is a good business opportunity for you?

_____

_____

_____

_____

_____

_____

Concepts Review

1. What is a business opportunity?

   _____

   _____

   _____

2. What are the five questions that begin the process of determining whether or not an idea might be a good business opportunity?

   _____

   _____

   _____

   _____

   _____

   _____

3. Given these hypothetical situations, name a business that you would consider starting or investing in:

   a. A 100% increase in the price of gasoline _____

   _____

   b. A going-out-of-business sign in the window of a local grocery store _____

   _____

   c. A new airport being built near your home _____

   _____

   d. An increase in the percentage of women entering the workforce _____

   _____

   e. Local government decides to privatize garbage collection and recycling collection.

   _____

   f. Government provides money to parents to spend as they wish on education for their

   children _____

STUDY GUIDE 6.2

4. What are three questions you should ask yourself before starting a new business?

_____

_____

_____

5. List three inventions and the consumer needs they filled.

_____

_____

_____

6. Would you go to the expense of making a prototype for a product you invented? Why or why not?

_____

_____

_____

7. List and briefly describe three practical methods for determining the feasibility of a business idea.

_____

_____

_____

_____

8. Prepare for the class Invention Contest by developing a new invention or a product improvement. On a separate sheet of paper, describe your invention briefly and include a drawing. Be sure to describe how your invention will meet a consumer need.

9. Write a two-page report about the life of a minority or woman inventor.

10. On a separate piece of paper, explain why you agree or disagree with this thought: "When you cease to dream, you cease to live."

11. Research an invention and write a paper describing how the inventor came up with the idea for the invention.

Crossword

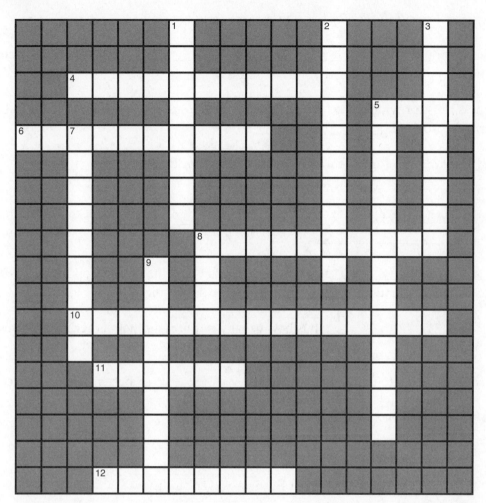

Use the clues below to solve the puzzle, which contains many vocabulary terms from Section 6.2.

Across

4. How possible or worthwhile a business idea is to pursue

5. Something people must have to survive

6. Quality that means being nonmaterial; something you cannot touch

8. Area that a SWOT analysis evaluates

10. Value of what you will give up to get something (2 words)

11. Someone licensed to sell businesses is a business _____

12. _____ thinking involves looking at a situation or object in new ways

Down

1. _____ thinking involves analyzing and evaluating a situation or object

2. Ongoing payment based on a percentage of sales a franchise earns (2 words)

3. Area that a SWOT analysis evaluates

5. Type of legal agreement you sign to keep certain information confidential

7. Convention where related businesses come to promote their products (2 words)

8. Product or service that people desire

9. Model on which reproductions of an invention are based

Check Yourself

In the sentences below, fill in the blanks with the correct answer.

1. A business should fill a _____ or _____ that is not currently being met.

2. A business must provide a product or service at a price that will attract customers but still earn a reasonable _____.

3. Critical thinking is a logical thought process that involves _____ and _____ a situation or object.

4. Creative thinking works well for generating _____ and recognizing _____.

5. An _____ cost analysis compares the benefits of one opportunity with the benefits of any opportunities you will be losing or postponing.

6. Buying an _____ business usually requires a much larger initial investment than starting a _____ business.

7. Some sources estimate that a franchise has a _____ or better chance of success.

Circle whether each statement is true or false.

8. True   False   Every business idea is a good opportunity.

9. True   False   Trade associations exist for nearly every industry.

10. True   False   A cost/benefit analysis evaluates the benefits of other opportunities.

11. True   False   Challenging the usual involves asking "Why?" and "What if?" questions.

12. True   False   Creative thinking must be done alone, not in a group.

13. True   False   Buying an existing business usually requires a large amount of money.

14. True   False   Inventors create new products or significantly change existing products.

Extend Your Knowledge

Research the Internet for information about trade associations and trade shows. Prepare a presentation for the class describing how these associations and shows can benefit entrepreneurs in choosing a business opportunity. Make sure your presentation is the length specified by the instructor.

STUDY GUIDE 6.2

STUDY GUIDE
Section 7.1

What Is Market Research?

Before You Begin

Think about the following question:

What are your three favorite ways to spend your free time?

Quickly write down your list. You don't have to place them in any special order.

_____

_____

_____

Describe any products or services that are involved in your three favorite free-time activities.

_____

_____

_____

_____

_____

_____

_____

_____

Could knowing how your classmates like to spend their free time be useful information to business owners in your area? Explain.

_____

_____

_____

_____

_____

_____

Concepts Review

STUDY GUIDE 7.1

1. What is market research?

_____

_____

_____

_____

_____

2. What three key areas should you research to help you understand your market?

_____

_____

_____

3. What are some costly mistakes that you can avoid by doing market research?

_____

_____

_____

_____

_____

_____

4. How does market research help entrepreneurs obtain finances?

_____

_____

_____

_____

_____

_____

5. What is the difference between B2C and B2B?

_____

_____

6. Name three ways that you can group customers into market segments.

_____

_____

_____

7. What is the difference between secondary data and primary data?

_____

_____

_____

_____

8. Name four sources of secondary data.

_____

_____

9. Name three techniques for collecting primary data.

_____

_____

_____

10. Think of a recording artist you like. Is this person a good entrepreneur? Is he or she setting or following trends? Is this artist aware enough of the market to stay on top?

_____

_____

_____

_____

_____

_____

Crossword

Use the clues below to solve the puzzle, which contains many vocabulary terms from Section 7.1.

Across

1. With 11 ACROSS, detailed description of a market's characteristics

5. Business _____ refers to any social, economic, or political factor that could impact a business

8. Market _____ is a group of consumers or businesses in a particular market with at least one thing in common

11. With 1 ACROSS, detailed description of a market's characteristics

12. New research information collected for a particular purpose (2 words)

13. Objective social and economic facts about people

14. Maximum number of companies an industry can support based on its potential customer base (2 words)

Down

2. Small number of people brought together to give feedback on a product or service (2 words)

3. Type of company that sells names and addresses for mailings (2 words)

4. Basing market segments on where consumers live or where businesses are located

6. What each "B" in B2B stands for

7. Psychological characteristics of consumers, such as opinions and personality

9. Limited number of customers who are most likely to buy a product or service (2 words)

10. What the "C" in B2C stands for

Name _____ Class_____ Date _____

Check Yourself

In the sentences below, fill in the blanks with the correct answer.

1. Market research helps you determine very specific _____ about potential customers.

2. Carrying capacity refers to the _____ number of companies that an industry can support based on its potential _____ base.

3. Demographic data is an example of _____ data.

4. Gathering primary data is more _____ and _____ than gathering secondary data.

5. Grouping customers into market segments based on where they live is called _____.

6. A _____ group is a source of primary market research data.

7. One of the purposes of market research is to help you avoid _____.

8. To be successful, businesses must satisfy their customers while making a _____.

Circle whether each statement is true or false.

9. True   False   Market research only needs to be done before starting a business.

10. True   False   Market research helps you identify who your competitors are.

11. True   False   A target market is smaller than a mass market.

12. True   False   Small businesses typically sell products and services to a mass market.

13. True   False   A target market can include more than one market segment.

14. True   False   Age, gender, and family size are psychographic data.

15. True   False   Secondary data is obtained directly from potential customers.

16. True   False   Gathering market research data can help you choose your target market.

Extend Your Knowledge

Use the Website of the U.S. Census Bureau to learn as much as you can about the demographics of the people living in your community. Prepare a paper detailing your findings. Include at least 3 tables or charts in your report that highlight data that might be of interest to potential business owners in your community. Make sure the paper is the length specified by the instructor.

STUDY GUIDE
Section 7.2

What Is Your Competitive Advantage?

Before You Begin

Think about the following question:

Is competition in business good?

Answer: ☐ **Yes**   ☐ **No**

If **Yes**, who benefits from competition between businesses?

_____

_____

_____

_____

_____

_____

If **No**, why is competition in business a bad thing?

_____

_____

_____

_____

_____

_____

What can a business owner do to make his or her business successful when there is a lot of competition?

_____

_____

_____

_____

_____

Concepts Review

1. Define "competitive advantage."

   _____

   _____

2. Pick three businesses you go to as a customer and describe their competitive advantages.

   _____

   _____

   _____

3. What is the difference between direct competitors and indirect competitors?

   _____

   _____

   _____

   _____

   _____

4. In order to succeed, does a company need to sell a product or service more cheaply than the competition? Explain your answer.

   _____

   _____

   _____

5. Describe some ways to gather competitive intelligence about a competitor.

   _____

   _____

   _____

   _____

   _____

6. How do you prepare a competitive matrix?

_____

_____

_____

7. Name three reasons for creating a competitive matrix.

_____

_____

_____

8. List four questions to help you identify potential differentiators for your business.

_____

_____

_____

_____

9. What is the purpose of an expanded SWOT analysis?

_____

_____

_____

_____

10. What are the six basic steps of market research that allow an entrepreneur to make a preliminary "go/no-go" decision about a business opportunity?

_____

_____

_____

11. What are four focus areas that can help you draw realistic conclusions about whether to proceed with your business idea?

_____

_____

Crossword

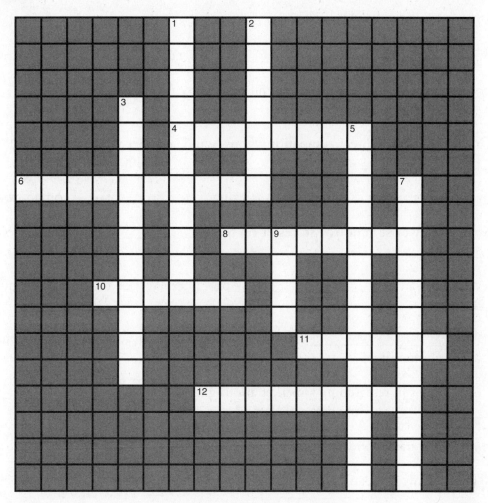

Use the clues below to solve the puzzle, which contains many vocabulary terms from Section 7.2.

Across

4. Use the _____ SWOT analysis to compare your business with competitor data

6. First basic step in market research is to identify research _____

8. Type of competitor that sells a different product from yours but fills the same customer need

10. McDonald's is a _____ competitor of Burger King

11. A competitive _____ is a grid that compares your business with your competitors'

12. Competitive _____ is something that puts a business ahead of the competition

Down

1. With 7 DOWN, the data you collect about your rival businesses

2. Area that a SWOT analysis evaluates

3. With 9 DOWN, the last basic step in market research

5. Unique characteristic that distinguishes one business from others

7. With 1 DOWN, the data you collect about your rival businesses

9. With 3 DOWN, the last basic step in market research

STUDY GUIDE 7.2

Check Yourself

In the sentences below, fill in the blanks with the correct answer.

1. Two pizza restaurants would be _____ competitors.

2. Your competitors are any businesses that fill the same customer _____ or _____ as your business.

3. When analyzing your indirect competition you should consider which groups will compete most _____ and most _____ with your business.

4. A competitive matrix is a useful tool for analyzing _____ competitors.

5. Competition may exist in nearby stores or on the _____ or in direct-mail _____.

6. A differentiator can be a _____ product or service that only your business offers.

7. One or more _____ can be the competitive advantage that puts your business ahead of the competition.

8. Three of the steps in researching a market are to gather data, _____ the data, and _____ the data.

Circle whether each statement is true or false.

9. True   False   Only companies that sell the same products as yours are your competitors.

10. True   False   A sandwich shop and a seafood restaurant are indirect competitors.

11. True   False   You will probably have more indirect competitors than direct competitors.

12. True   False   Direct competitors should be analyzed in groups rather than individually.

13. True   False   Your competitive advantage could consist of one or more differentiators.

14. True   False   Differentiators are characteristics that businesses have in common.

15. True   False   Once you have a competitive advantage you will always have it.

16. True   False   Step 1 of market research is identifying what you want to accomplish.

Extend Your Knowledge

Use the Internet to research a successful company that has used differentiation to create a competitive advantage for itself. Prepare a presentation for the class describing the differentiators and how the company used them to set itself apart from its competitors. Make sure the presentation is the length specified by the instructor.

STUDY GUIDE
Section 8.1

Developing Your Marketing Mix

Before You Begin

Think about the following question:

Is the brand of a product important?

List five product types that you regularly purchase—for example, athletic shoes or hair gel.

_____

_____

For each product category list all the brands you can think for that category. For example, Nike is a brand of athletic shoes.

Product Category	Brand

Do you consider the brand when you purchase these products? Why or why not?

_____

_____

_____

_____

_____

Name _____ Class _____ Date _____

Concepts Review

STUDY GUIDE 8.1

1. Name seven factors to consider when setting your marketing goals.

   _____

   _____

   _____

2. How is market share calculated?

   _____

   _____

3. What are the "Five P's" that make up a marketing mix?

   _____

4. Who are the two groups of people you should consider in your marketing mix?

   _____

5. What are some factors to consider when you are trying to attract customers to your product?

   _____

   _____

6. How does branding help to maintain customer loyalty?

   _____

   _____

   _____

7. What factors should you consider in the packaging of your product?

   _____

   _____

   _____

   _____

8. What is the difference between a direct distribution channel and an indirect distribution channel?

_____

_____

_____

_____

9. Name the three basic arrangements through which products are distributed to sales outlets.

_____

_____

10. List four sample price objectives.

_____

_____

_____

11. Name three basic pricing strategies.

_____

_____

12. When and why are markup prices and markdown prices used to make price adjustments?

_____

_____

_____

_____

_____

_____

13. Name some factors that service businesses use to determine prices for their services.

_____

_____

_____

STUDY GUIDE 8.1

Crossword

Use the clues below to solve the puzzle, which contains many vocabulary terms from Section 8.1.

Across

2. Reason customers choose to buy a product

5. Another name for 14 ACROSS

9. Price adjustment a retailer makes to reduce the cost of a product

10. Combination of items a business sells (2 words)

11. Market _____ is the percentage of people from a given market who buy your product or service

12. Pricing method focused on how much consumers will pay for a product (2 words)

14. Symbol used to identify a product (2 words)

Down

1. Process used to make people aware of and interested in buying your product or service

3. What a product does and how it appears to the senses

4. Detailed guide that describes goals and strategies for presenting your business (2 words)

6. Combining the price of several services or products into one price

7. Pricing method focused on what you pay to produce a product (2 words)

8. Type of distribution that makes a product available in as many locations as possible

13. Price adjustment a retailer makes to the wholesale cost to make a profit

Check Yourself

In the sentences below, fill in the blanks with the correct answer.

1. The two primary parts of your marketing plan are your _____ and your _____ for reaching your goals.

2. Building a product image involves attracting _____ customers and building _____ among existing customers.

3. A marketing mix is created by combining the _____.

4. An intermediary is present in an _____ distribution channel.

5. Appearance and scent are examples of the _____ of a product.

6. Making a product available at many sales outlets is called _____ distribution.

7. The price of your product should be based on your target _____ and the potential _____ for your business.

8. Demand-based pricing is most appropriate when customers perceive your product as _____ or having greater _____ than similar products.

Circle whether each statement is true or false.

9. True   False   All businesses have the same marketing goals.

10. True   False   Marketing goals should have a time frame.

11. True   False   A marketing mix is a combination of the Five P's.

12. True   False   Product features and benefits can attract customers to your product.

13. True   False   The purpose of branding is to build employee loyalty.

14. True   False   Distribution channels are one component of place strategies.

15. True   False   The benefits of a product are based on how it appears to the senses.

16. True   False   Cost-based pricing focuses on your competitors' prices for a product.

Extend Your Knowledge

Using Internet resources research the common components of a marketing plan. Create an outline for a basic marketing plan and present it to the class in a PowerPoint presentation. Briefly describe each component of the outline and explain why it should be included in the marketing plan. Make sure your presentation is the length specified by the instructor.

STUDY GUIDE 8.1

STUDY GUIDE
Section 8.2

Promoting Your Product

Before You Begin

Think about the following question:

Do you always believe advertisements?

Answer: ☐ **Yes**   ☐ **No**

List all the formats and types of advertisements that come to mind.

_____

_____

_____

_____

_____

_____

Do you believe some advertisements and not others? Explain.

_____

_____

_____

_____

_____

_____

Do advertisements ever influence your decisions? Why or why not?

_____

_____

_____

_____

_____

_____

Concepts Review

1. Name and briefly define the four components of AIDA.

   _____

   _____

   _____

   _____

2. List the six elements of a promotional mix.

   _____

   _____

   _____

3. Name the six most common types of advertising.

   _____

   _____

   _____

4. Define visual merchandising.

   _____

   _____

5. List three activities and tools that PR staff can use to get publicity for your business.

   _____

   _____

6. Name some of the methods and places your sales staff might use to meet and/or communicate with customers in an informal person-to-person manner.

   _____

   _____

   _____

   _____

STUDY GUIDE 8.2

7. What are the three stages of a promotional plan for a business startup?

_____

_____

_____

_____

8. What should be included in each promotional campaign?

_____

_____

_____

_____

9. Why is it important to measure the effectiveness of your promotions?

_____

_____

_____

_____

10. Name the four factors that will determine your promotional budget.

_____

_____

_____

_____

11. List three low-cost promotional strategies.

_____

_____

_____

Crossword

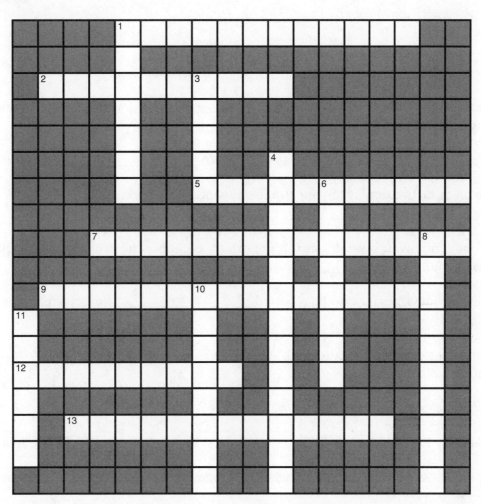

Use the clues below to solve the puzzle, which contains many vocabulary terms from Section 8.2

Across

1. Written statement about a business that you send out to get publicity (2 words)

2. Brochures, print catalogs, and sales letters are examples of this (2 words)

5. Public promotional message paid for by an identified company

7. Activities aimed at creating goodwill toward a product or company (2 words)

9. Practice of having an actor use a brand-name item in a TV show or movie (2 words)

12. Online message board where people post information about a topic

13. Visual _____ is using artistic displays to attract customers into a store

Down

1. Giveaway item that has a company's name printed on it

3. Communication channels, such as newspapers, TV, and radio

4. Selling products or services over the phone

6. Strategy of swapping your company's product or service for radio air time

8. Technique used for meeting new people to find new customers

10. CPM stands for cost-per-_____

11. Web _____ is an advertisement embedded on a Website

Check Yourself

In the sentences below, fill in the blanks with the correct answer.

1. AIDA is a communications model used by businesses to _____, _____, and _____ their promotions.

2. The purpose of promotion is to build a _____ awareness about your product and business and to influence people to _____ your product.

3. An ad placed in a school yearbook is an example of _____ advertising.

4. Having an attractive display in your storefront window is an example of _____.

5. When budgeting your promotions it is important to choose the promotional media that will best reach your _____ audience.

6. Promotional messages have to be repeated _____ times to maximize their effectiveness.

7. It is important to include methods for measuring promotion _____ in your promotional plan.

Circle whether each statement is true or false.

8. True False Researching advertising rates is part of setting a promotional budget.

9. True False A promotional mix includes only one form of promotion.

10. True False Advertising helps build a brand's image.

11. True False The Internet cannot be used to promote a product.

12. True False Publicity is an expensive type of advertising.

13. True False 360° marketing uses both low-tech and high-tech methods of communication.

14. True False A promotional plan is needed even before a business is opened.

Extend Your Knowledge

Web banners (or banner ads) are a popular form of Internet advertising. Write a how-to guide for new entrepreneurs interested in using Web banners to bring visitors to their Web sites. Explain how and why the ads are used and their advantages and disadvantages. Make sure your guide is the length specified by the instructor.

STUDY GUIDE
Section 9.1

Principles of Successful Selling

Before You Begin

Think about the following question:

Are you a good salesperson?

Answer: ☐ Yes ☐ No

If **Yes**, explain what makes you a good salesperson.

_____

_____

_____

_____

_____

_____

If **No**, explain why you believe you are not a good salesperson.

_____

_____

_____

_____

_____

_____

What are the characteristics of a good salesperson?

_____

_____

_____

_____

_____

_____

Concepts Review

1. What is personal selling?

   _____

   _____

   _____

   _____

2. What are the advantages of personal selling compared to other types of promotion?

   _____

   _____

   _____

   _____

3. Name the six characteristics of successful salespeople.

   _____

   _____

4. What is the selling process?

   _____

   _____

   _____

   _____

   _____

5. List the four main steps in the selling process.

   _____

   _____

   _____

   _____

6. Name four common ways that sales leads can be obtained.

_____

_____

7. What is the difference between a sales lead and a prospect?

_____

_____

_____

_____

_____

8. What five things should you do to prepare for a sales call on a prospect?

_____

_____

_____

_____

_____

9. List five suggestions for making sales calls more successful.

_____

_____

_____

_____

_____

10. Name five documents or forms that are helpful in the mechanics of selling.

_____

_____

_____

_____

_____

STUDY GUIDE 9.1

Crossword

Use the clues below to solve the puzzle, which contains many vocabulary terms from Section 9.1.

Across

4. Reasons a customer may be cautious about buying

7. Using a computer to search collections of electronic information for sales trends (2 words)

11. Person or company that has some characteristics of your target market (2 words)

12. Connection between people based on mutual respect and trust

13. With 8 DOWN, upbeat characteristic of a successful salesperson

14. What 11 ACROSS might become: a potential customer

Down

1. What you do after closing a sale to keep a new customer happy (2 words)

2. Potential customer recommended to you by someone else

3. What you have to ask for to close a sale

5. To contact in person or by phone in order to qualify someone as a potential customer (2 words)

6. Descriptive list produced by a cash register at the time of a sale

8. With 13 ACROSS, upbeat characteristic of a successful salesperson

9. To contact a stranger, without prior notice, in order to make a sale (2 words)

10. What the "P" in RFP stands for

Name _____Class_____Date _____

Check Yourself

In the sentences below, fill in the blanks with the correct answer.

1. Options for personal selling include face-to-face meetings, phone conversations, and _____.

2. Successful salespeople have a _____ attitude and are _____ listeners.

3. To be consistent means to be _____ and to keep in touch with _____.

4. A qualified sales lead becomes a _____.

5. Referrals often come from _____ existing customers.

6. Data mining involves using a _____ to search databases.

7. Asking for a commitment is an important part of _____ the sale.

8. A _____ is a record of telephone calls made to prospects.

Circle whether each statement is true or false.

9. True   False   A salesperson is more likely to sell to a prospect than to a sales lead.

10. True   False   Building rapport with customers is bad for business.

11. True   False   Cold calling is trying to sell something to people you do not know.

12. True   False   Salespeople often make a sale to their first contact.

13. True   False   An RFP is issued by a business interested in buying something.

14. True   False   Successful salespeople interrupt their customers a lot.

15. True   False   Personal selling is a good way to deal with customer objections.

16. True   False   Every sales lead turns into a prospect.

Extend Your Knowledge

Imagine you are a salesperson for a successful business that creates Websites. Search the Internet for a Website you believe needs improving. The Website could belong to a company, charity, or other organization (even your own school). Pretend your classmates are the owners of the Website, and you are making a sales call on them. Give them a PowerPoint presentation in which you try to convince them to let your company redesign their Website. Make sure your presentation is the length specified by the instructor.

STUDY GUIDE 9.2

STUDY GUIDE
Section 9.2

Estimating Sales

Before You Begin

Think about the following question:

Why would a company need to estimate its future sales?

What plans do you and your family make based on income you expect in the near future?

_____

_____

_____

_____

What factors could you predict that might negatively or positively affect this future income?

_____

_____

_____

_____

How will your plans change as your income forecast changes?

_____

_____

_____

_____

Why would a company need to estimate its future sales?

_____

_____

_____

_____

Concepts Review

1. What five questions should you ask yourself when you perform sales force planning?

   _____

   _____

   _____

   _____

   _____

2. What are the advantages and disadvantages of using external selling methods?

   _____

   _____

   _____

   _____

   _____

   _____

   _____

   _____

3. What are the advantages and disadvantages of using internal selling methods?

   _____

   _____

   _____

   _____

4. Describe three common roles of a sales force.

   _____

   _____

   _____

   _____

Name _____Class_____Date _____

STUDY GUIDE 9.2

5. List three ways in which salespeople are commonly paid.

_____

_____

6. What is the difference between a sales quota and a sales territory?

_____

_____

_____

7. Name five subjects commonly taught in company sales-training programs.

_____

_____

_____

8. What are some of the miscellaneous expenses associated with a sales force?

_____

_____

9. Why is sales forecasting important?

_____

_____

_____

10. List the four general steps to preparing a sales forecast.

_____

_____

_____

11. Name eight common sales-forecasting techniques.

_____

_____

_____

Crossword

Use the clues below to solve the puzzle, which contains many vocabulary terms from Section 9.2.

Across

1. Targeted number of sales per month that a salesperson is expected to achieve

5. Fixed amount of money paid to an employee on a regular basis

7. Amount paid to a salesperson based on the volume of products sold

8. _____ sales force is made of employees who work for the company full time

11. Sales _____ is a salesperson's geographical area of responsibility

12. Type of sales obtained by hiring another company to do the selling for you

14. To predict sales, gather _____ data by monitoring your competitors' customers

Down

2. Sales role that involves finding prospects, presenting the product, and closing the sale (2 words)

3. Positions that involve assisting others with selling activities (2 words)

4. A sales _____ predicts future sales over a period of time

6. Type of sales made by only you or your employees

9. Sales role that involves processing sales from customers who seek out a product (2 words)

10. Sales _____ apply to some industries, causing stronger sales during certain seasons

13. Sales _____ helps new employees gain knowledge and skills

Name _____ Class_____ Date _____

Check Yourself

In the sentences below, fill in the blanks with the correct answer.

1. Sales force planning should be performed as you develop and refine your _____.

2. The _____ provides a way to successfully sell your products and services with fewer salespeople.

3. Most salespeople are paid a combination of _____ and _____.

4. Your salespeople should be knowledgeable about your company and the _____ it sells.

5. Your salespeople should know the characteristics of your target _____.

6. Sales forecasts for established companies are based on _____ sales.

7. Observational data is obtained by observing your competitors' _____.

8. Sales forecasts for retail stores are sometimes based on sales per _____.

Circle whether each statement is true or false.

9. True   False   A sales forecast is an estimate.

10. True   False   The clerk that rings up your groceries at the store is an order getter.

11. True   False   Technology skills for salespeople may involve computer programs.

12. True   False   Salespeople need to learn as much about the competition as possible.

13. True   False   Paying a salesperson only a salary motivates him or her to sell a lot.

14. True   False   External salespeople and sales agents are employees of your business.

15. True   False   A full-capacity forecast predicts you will sell everything you produce.

16. True   False   Seasonal sales cycles are often associated with holidays.

Extend Your Knowledge

Sales forecasting can be very mathematical. Use Internet resources to learn about two mathematical terms—trend lines and variables—that are associated with sales forecasting. Write a report describing what you learn. Include several examples and at least two charts or graphs to help your readers understand the concepts involved. Make sure your report is the length specified by the instructor.

STUDY GUIDE
Section 10.1

The Cost of Doing Business

Before You Begin

Think about the following question:

Why do businesses need to control their expenses?

If profit equals sales minus expenses, then what happens when expenses are reduced?

_____

_____

_____

_____

_____

What can a business owner do with profit?

_____

_____

_____

_____

_____

Why do businesses need to control their expenses?

_____

_____

_____

_____

_____

_____

_____

Concepts Review

1. How are expenses related to profit?

_____

_____

_____

2. Explain why fixed expenses do not change in response to sales.

_____

_____

_____

3. List the eight most common fixed expenses and the phrase that helps you remember them.

_____

_____

_____

_____

4. What is depreciation?

_____

_____

_____

5. What is the formula used in the straight-line method of depreciation?

_____

_____

_____

_____

6. Give two examples of fixed expenses that can change.

_____

_____

_____

_____

7. Define variable expense.

_____

_____

_____

_____

8. What is Cost of Goods Sold (COGS) and what does it include?

_____

_____

_____

_____

_____

_____

9. What is economy of scale?

_____

_____

_____

_____

10. What are the two most common ways for a business to benefit from economy of scale?

_____

_____

_____

_____

Crossword

Use the clues below to solve the puzzle, which contains many vocabulary terms from Section 10.1.

Across

4. With 7 DOWN, estimate of what equipment can be sold for at the end of its business life

6. Accounting method of spreading the cost of equipment over a number of years of use

8. A common fixed business expense (the "U" in "I SAID U ROX")

10. A common fixed business expense (the "S" in "I SAID U ROX")

11. Spreading expenses over a large amount of goods is called _____ of scale

13. Type of expense that changes based on the amount of product or service a business sells

14. Expense that isn't affected by the number of items a business produces (2 words)

Down

1. Method of depreciation that estimates how long equipment will last and how much it can be sold for (2 words)

2. A common fixed business expense (the "A" in "I SAID U ROX")

3. Type of discount you get when you buy in quantity

5. What the "GS" in COGS stands for (2 words)

7. With 4 ACROSS, estimate of what equipment can be sold for at the end of its life

9. A common fixed business expense (the "I" in "I SAID U ROX")

12. A common fixed business expense (the "R" in "I SAID U ROX")

Name _____Class_____Date _____

Check Yourself

In the sentences below, fill in the blanks with the correct answer.

1. A business can only make a profit if all of the expenses associated with a product or service are _____ than the selling price for that product or service.

2. Fixed expenses are regular ongoing expenses that a business must pay to be able to _____.

3. Fixed expenses _____ include expenses directly related to the products the business sells.

4. Total depreciation is the difference between an item's actual cost and its _____.

5. The _____ expense is the cost per year to a business of having the use of a particular piece of equipment.

6. Expenses that vary with the amount of product sold are called _____.

7. The cost of _____ and _____ used to make a product are variable expenses.

8. Typically in business the cost per unit _____ as you buy larger amounts.

Circle whether each statement is true or false.

9. True   False   Every sale has related expenses.

10. True   False   Fixed expenses increase when the number of products sold increases.

11. True   False   The monthly cost of Internet access is an example of a fixed expense.

12. True   False   The phrase for remembering fixed expenses is U SAID E ROX.

13. True   False   If your rent goes up then rent is no longer a fixed expense.

14. True   False   Salvage value is what an item sells for at the end of its business life.

15. True   False   Sales commissions and packaging expenses are variable expenses.

16. True   False   Volume discount means you pay less per item when you buy fewer items.

Extend Your Knowledge

Henry Ford is famous for reducing costs and using economy of scale in his automobile business. Write a paper explaining how Ford accomplished these things and how they benefited him, his company, his employees, and consumers of the early 1900s. Make sure your paper is the length specified by the instructor.

STUDY GUIDE
Section 10.2

The Economics of One Unit of Sale

Before You Begin

Think about the following question:

Would you want to know how much profit you made every time you sold a pair of shoes.

Answer: ☐ **Yes** ☐ **No**

If **Yes**, why is it important for you to know the profit you make on each pair of shoes?

_____

_____

_____

_____

_____

If **No**, why is it not important for you to know the profit you make on each pair of shoes?

_____

_____

_____

_____

_____

Does each pair of shoes you sell have a cost to you? Explain.

_____

_____

_____

_____

_____

Name _____ Class _____ Date _____

Concepts Review

1. Define unit of sale.

_____

_____

_____

2. Explain why a unit of sale is not the same for every business.

_____

_____

_____

_____

3. How do you calculate the contribution margin?

_____

_____

_____

4. How do you calculate the EOU for a manufacturing business (vs. other types of businesses)?

_____

_____

_____

_____

5. How do you calculate the EOU for a retail business (vs. other types of businesses)?

_____

_____

_____

_____

6. How do you calculate the EOU for a service business (vs. other types of businesses)?

_____

_____

_____

_____

7. List four options for determining the cost per unit for a range of similar products.

_____

_____

_____

_____

8. How is Cost of Services Sold calculated for the service business that does not use supplies to perform the service?

_____

_____

_____

9. How is Cost of Services Sold calculated for a service business that uses supplies to perform the service?

_____

_____

_____

_____

10. If the owner of a service business doesn't actually provide the service, can the owner make money?

_____

_____

_____

_____

Crossword

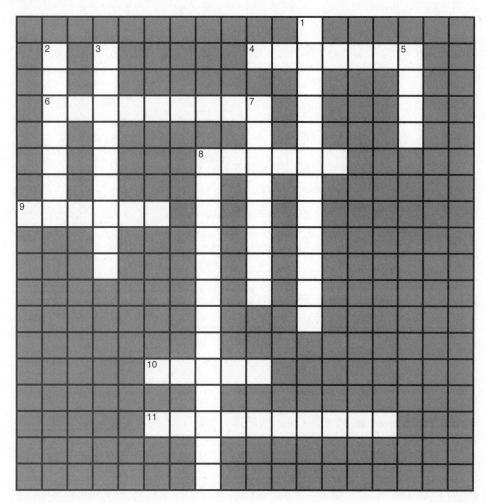

Use the clues below to solve the puzzle, which contains many vocabulary terms from Section 10.2.

Across

4. Selling price minus expenses equals _____

6. What the "E" of EOU stands for

8. With 1 DOWN, the amount per unit that can be applied toward a company's profitability before subtracting fixed expenses

9. The EOU of this type of business includes commissions

10. To calculate the EOU of a service business, you must factor in the number of _____ it takes to perform the service

11. Amount of product you use to figure your operations and profit (3 words)

Down

1. With 8 ACROSS, the amount per unit that can be applied toward a company's profitability before subtracting fixed expenses

2. To calculate the EOU of a business selling multiple products, you can use the _____ cost of the products

3. The EOU of this type of business does not include labor

5. What the second "S" in "COSS" stands for

7. What the first "S" in "COSS" stands for

8. The EOU of this type of business includes labor

Check Yourself

In the sentences below, fill in the blanks with the correct answer.

1. The purpose of the EOU is to determine the amount of profit a business makes every time it sells _____ item.

2. The unit of sale for a retailer selling shoes is _____ of shoes.

3. The economics of one unit is calculated by subtracting the _____ of the unit from the _____ of the unit.

4. The contribution margin is the amount per unit a product contributes toward the company's _____ before the _____ are subtracted.

5. The Cost of Goods Sold for a manufacturing business includes the cost for _____ and _____.

6. A typical EOU for a line of similar products could be calculated based on the average _____ of the products.

7. A service business uses the Cost of _____ Sold to calculate its EOU.

8. COGS and COSS are both _____ expenses.

Circle whether each statement is true or false.

9. True False Labor costs are included in the EOU calculation for a retailer.

10. True False A unit of sale for a wholesaler could be a carton containing many items.

11. True False The contribution margin considers variable and fixed expenses.

12. True False The supplies used to provide a service are a variable expense.

13. True False Labor costs are included in the EOU calculation for a wholesaler.

14. True False A unit of sale is the largest unit that the customer can actually buy.

15. True False Labor costs are included in the EOU calculation for a manufacturer.

Extend Your Knowledge

Use the Internet to research how existing businesses use a contribution-margin analysis to compare the performance of different products or different product lines. Present your findings to the class in a PowerPoint presentation including at least one table as an example. Also discuss how a new entrepreneur might be able to use a contribution-margin analysis to choose from a variety of products or services that he or she is considering selling. Make sure your presentation is the length specified by the instructor.

Name _____ Class _____ Date _____

STUDY GUIDE
Section 11.1

Income Statements & Cash Flow

Before You Begin

Think about the following question:

Is it important for an entrepreneur to know basic accounting principles?

Answer: ☐ Yes ☐ No

What is accounting?

_____

_____

_____

_____

_____

_____

How is accounting used by businesses?

_____

_____

_____

_____

_____

_____

Why should an entrepreneur know basic accounting principles?

_____

_____

_____

_____

_____

Concepts Review

1. List the three category headings used on an income statement for variable expenses, and list the type of business that uses each.

   _____

   _____

   _____

2. What is the difference between a traditional-format income statement and a contribution-margin-format income statement for a merchandising business?

   _____

   _____

   _____

3. Name the six parts of a typical income statement for a manufacturing business.

   _____

   _____

4. List the five parts of a cash flow statement.

   _____

   _____

5. Name five ways that a business owner can keep cash flowing into a business.

   _____

   _____

   _____

6. Explain a burn rate and the calculation in which it is used.

   _____

   _____

   _____

   _____

7. You have a business selling caps to friends and classmates. This June you bought 20 caps for $5 each and sold them all at $10 each. You paid $40 in commissions to your brother to help you sell them, and you spent $20 on posters as advertising. Your taxes are 20% of your pre-tax profit. Prepare your income statement.

Income Statement

Month _____

REVENUE

Gross Sales $ _____

Sales Returns   _____

Net Sales $ _____

COST OF GOODS MANUFACTURED AND SOLD

Materials $ _____

Labor   _____

Total Cost of Goods Sold   _____

GROSS PROFIT $ _____

OPERATING EXPENSES

Advertising $ _____

Commissions   _____

Depreciation   _____

Insurance   _____

Rent   _____

Utilities   _____

Salaries   _____

Total Expenses   _____

PRE-TAX PROFIT $ _____

Taxes (20%)   _____

NET PROFIT $ _____

Crossword

Use the clues below to solve the puzzle, which contains many vocabulary terms from Section 11.1.

Across

2. The _____ rate determines how long a business can go without earning revenue

5. A business can _____ equipment to conserve cash

6. Accounting period that goes from Jan. 1–Dec. 31 is a(n) _____ year

9. With 4 DOWN, this type of income statement subtracts variable expenses from net sales

10. Any 12-month period used for accounting purposes is a(n) _____ year

11. Money spent to buy inventory is called cash _____

12. On an income statement, the costs of running a business are _____ expenses

Down

1. This is calculated by subtracting the cost of items sold from net sales (2 words)

3. Describes the selling period for seasonal businesses

4. With 9 ACROSS, this type of income statement subtracts variable expenses from net sales

7. The Red Cross is an example of this type of organization

8. Money received minus what is spent over a specified period of time (2 words)

13. Income statement for retailers shows the cost of _____ sold

Name _____ Class_____ Date _____

Check Yourself

In the sentences below, fill in the blanks with the correct answer.

1. An income statement shows a profit if a business's sales are _____ than its expenses.

2. The three components of revenue for a merchandising business are _____, _____, and _____.

3. The two components of cost of goods manufactured and sold are _____ and _____.

4. Gross profit for a service business is _____ minus the cost of _____ sold.

5. Net cash is calculated by subtracting _____ from _____.

6. A burn rate is typically expressed in terms of _____ spent per _____.

7. Net profit is calculated by subtracting _____ from pre-tax profit.

8. An income statement is also called a _____ and _____ statement.

Circle whether each statement is true or false.

9. True   False   At first, most small businesses should create an income statement monthly.

10. True   False   A fiscal year can be different from a calendar year.

11. True   False   All income statements include revenue, expenses, and net income or loss.

12. True   False   Gross profit for a retailer is net sales minus cost of services sold.

13. True   False   The operating expenses for a manufacturer include the cost of materials.

14. True   False   An income statement shows the amount of cash a business has on hand.

15. True   False   A cash flow statement should be prepared monthly.

16. True   False   Most new businesses earn more money than they spend at first.

Extend Your Knowledge

Every businessperson needs to know how to spot counterfeit money. Use Internet resources to learn about this topic. Present a talk about your findings. Include at least five specific tips for identifying counterfeit cash. Make sure your talk is the length specified by the instructor.

STUDY GUIDE
Section 11.2

The Balance Sheet

Before You Begin

Think about the following question:

If you owned a business, would you want to know its value?

Answer:　☐ **Yes**　　☐ **No**

If **Yes**, why is it important to know the value of your business?

_____

_____

_____

_____

_____

_____

If **No**, why is it not important to know the value of your business?

_____

_____

_____

_____

_____

_____

_____

How do you think the value of a business is determined?

_____

_____

_____

_____

_____

Concepts Review

1. What is the purpose of a balance sheet?

   _____

   _____

   _____

   _____

2. Explain each term in this equation: Assets – Liabilities = Owner's Equity.

   _____

   _____

   _____

   _____

3. Explain the difference between current assets and long-term assets.

   _____

   _____

   _____

   _____

4. Name some examples of current assets and long-term assets.

   _____

   _____

   _____

   _____

5. Explain the difference between current liabilities and long-term liabilities.

   _____

   _____

   _____

   _____

STUDY GUIDE 11.2

6. Name some examples of current liabilities and long-term liabilities.

_____

_____

_____

_____

_____

7. Describe the two main sections of a balance sheet.

_____

_____

_____

8. What are the five main accounts commonly included on a balance sheet?

_____

_____

9. When do businesses prepare the balance sheets that they use to determine how they have performed from year to year?

_____

_____

10. What is the purpose of preparing a comparative balance sheet?

_____

_____

_____

_____

11. How does a same-size balance sheet analysis differ from a standard comparative balance sheet analysis?

_____

_____

_____

Crossword

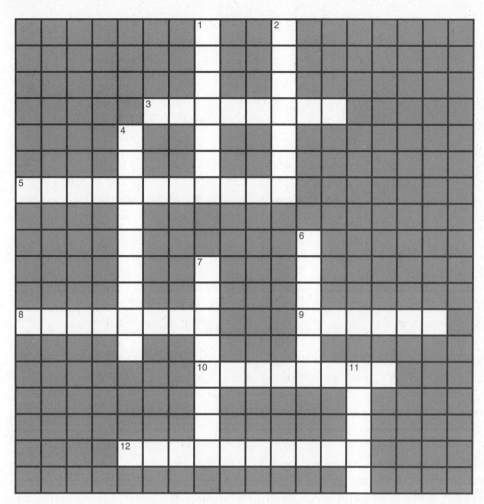

Use the clues below to solve the puzzle, which contains many vocabulary terms from Section 11.2.

Across

3. One type of loan that takes longer than a year to repay

5. Type of balance sheet that shows only the current year and the previous year

8. Type of 11 DOWN that takes longer than a year to turn into cash (2 words)

9. With 6 DOWN, the value of a business on a specific date

10. An amount owed to the state for merchandise sold (2 words)

12. Accounts _____ is the amount of money owed to a business for credit sales

Down

1. Type of 11 DOWN that can be converted into cash within one year

2. Accounts _____ is the amount of money a business owes for credit purchases

4. An outstanding bill or loan that must be repaid

6. With 9 ACROSS, the value of a business on a specific date

7. Type of balance sheet that shows the changes from one year to another as a percentage (2 words)

11. Item of value owned by a business

Check Yourself

In the sentences below, fill in the blanks with the correct answer.

1. A balance sheet shows how much a business is _____ on a specific _____.

2. Owner's equity is the value of a business if all the _____ were sold and all the _____ were paid.

3. Cash is a _____ asset, and machinery is a _____ asset.

4. Current liabilities include debts owed to suppliers, which are also called accounts _____.

5. All the assets of a business are listed in the _____ section of an income statement.

6. A comparative balance sheet compares balance sheets prepared on the _____ day of the fiscal year and the _____ day of the fiscal year.

7. A same-size balance sheet shows changes from last year to this year as a _____ of _____ year's amounts.

8. A balance sheet answers the questions: What does the company _____? And to whom does it owe _____?

Circle whether each statement is true or false

9. True   False   Owner's equity is the amount of money the entrepreneur gets to keep.

10. True   False   Liabilities are items of value that a business owns.

11. True   False   Long-term assets can be converted to cash within one year.

12. True   False   Owner's equity equals total liabilities minus total assets.

13. True   False   A mortgage is typically a long-term liability for a business.

14. True   False   Accounts receivable is money owed to others.

15. True   False   A comparative balance sheet shows changes in a business's value.

Extend Your Knowledge

Owner's equity in a business is much like homeowner's equity in a home. Write a paper explaining how these two concepts are similar. Explain how equity is valuable to a business owner and to a homeowner. Make sure your paper is the length specified by the instructor.

Name _____ Class _____ Date _____

STUDY GUIDE
Section 12.1

Financial Ratios

Before You Begin

Think about the following question:

How much profit should a company make? How much debt should a company have?

_____

What happens to a company's profits when it has a lot of debt to pay off?

_____

_____

_____

_____

_____

How much profit should a company make?

_____

_____

_____

_____

_____

_____

How much debt should a company have?

_____

_____

_____

_____

_____

Concepts Review

STUDY GUIDE 12.1

1. Describe financial ratios and how they are used.

_____

_____

_____

2. How is a sales-data analysis useful?

_____

_____

_____

3. How is a same-size analysis useful?

_____

_____

_____

4. How is an operating ratio calculated, and how is it used?

_____

_____

_____

5. How is return on sales calculated, and what does it show?

_____

_____

6. How is a debt ratio calculated?

_____

7. How is a debt-to-equity ratio calculated?

_____

_____

8. Describe a quick ratio.

_____

_____

9. Describe a current ratio.

_____

_____

10. How is return on investment calculated, and what does it show?

_____

_____

_____

11. What is the return on investment if a person invests $100 and makes a profit of $150?

_____

12. How much interest will be earned on $1,000 invested for one year at 6%?

_____

13. Complete the chart below. Assume a one-year investment period.

Return on Investment (ROI)		
Net Profit	Investment	ROI
$ 4	$ _____	100%
30	60	_____ %
25	100	_____ %
4	10	_____ %
10	_____	20%
4,000	_____	40%
2,000	_____	200%
_____	20,000	6%

Crossword

Use the clues below to solve the puzzle, which contains many vocabulary terms from Section 12.1.

Across

2. With 5 DOWN, the percentage of each dollar of revenue needed to cover expenses

4. Ratio that is found by dividing a business's present assets by its liabilities

6. Ability to convert assets into cash

10. With 3 DOWN, another name for investments, such as stocks or bonds, that can be converted to cash quickly

11. Portion of a pie chart

12. Ratio used to monitor the liabilities of a business

13. What "ROS" stands for (3 words)

Down

1. What "ROI" stands for (3 words)

3. With 10 ACROSS, another name for investments, such as stocks or bonds, that can be converted to cash quickly

5. With 2 ACROSS, the percentage of each dollar of revenue needed to cover expenses

7. A bar _____ uses vertical or horizontal bars to show data

8. Analysis that compares total revenue against that same data converted into percentages (2 words)

9. Ratio calculated by adding the value of a business's investments to the cash on hand

Check Yourself

In the sentences below, fill in the blanks with the correct answer.

1. Financial ratios are expressed as _____ or as _____.

2. A sales-data analysis can be used to forecast future _____.

3. The sales-data analysis, same-size analysis, operating ratio, and return on sales are all based on data in the _____.

4. The debt ratio, debt-to-equity ratio, quick ratio, and current ratio are all based on data in the _____.

5. The return on investment is calculated by dividing _____ by initial investment and multiplying by _____.

6. Operating ratios are used to compare companies within a particular _____.

7. A debt ratio of 25% means that the debts of the business equal _____ of its total assets.

Circle whether each statement is true or false.

8. True   False   An entrepreneur needs only one ratio to determine if a business is healthy.

9. True   False   A same-size analysis can compare income statements from different years.

10. True   False   Another name for return on sales is debt margin.

11. True   False   The quick ratio and current ratio help track the liquidity of a business.

12. True   False   The ROI divides current assets by the net profit.

13. True   False   Financial ratios show relationships, patterns, and trends in data.

14. True   False   The debt ratio and debt-to-equity ratios are calculated as percentages.

Extend Your Knowledge

Many large companies produce a colorful and reader-friendly report called an annual report in which they provide information about their company for the general public and investors. These reports typically include some financial statements, such as balance sheets, income statements, and cash flow statements. Use the Internet to find an annual report for a company in which you are interested. Use financial data in the report to prepare at least 2 pie charts and 2 bar charts not already included in the report. Prepare a paper to accompany the charts in which you explain how the charts were prepared and what they show. Include copies of the original data so your teacher can check your work. Make sure your paper is the length specified by the instructor.

STUDY GUIDE 12.2

STUDY GUIDE
Section 12.2

Break-Even Analysis

Before You Begin

Think about the following question:

How do you know if a business is profitable?

_____

Can you tell from sales data alone whether a business is profitable? Explain.

_____

_____

_____

_____

_____

Where does the money come from each month to pay a business's expenses?

_____

_____

_____

_____

_____

How do you know if a business is profitable?

_____

_____

_____

_____

_____

Concepts Review

1. What is a break-even point?

_____

_____

_____

_____

2. Describe a break-even analysis.

_____

_____

_____

_____

_____

3. What are some actions an entrepreneur can take if his or her business is not selling enough to pay all its expenses.

_____

_____

_____

_____

_____

4. Explain how total revenue is calculated in the break-even analysis for Matt's Hats.

_____

_____

5. Explain how Cost of Goods Sold is calculated in the break-even analysis for Matt's Hats.

_____

_____

_____

_____

STUDY GUIDE 12.2

6. Explain how total gross profit is calculated in the break-even analysis for Matt's Hats.

_____

_____

_____

7. Explain how gross profit per unit is calculated in the break-even analysis for Matt's Hats.

_____

_____

_____

8. What formula is used to calculate contribution margin per unit for a company with variable expenses other than the Cost of Goods Sold?

_____

_____

9. What are break-even units?

_____

_____

10. How are break-even units calculated for a traditional-format income statement?

_____

_____

_____

11. How are break-even units calculated for a contribution-margin-format income statement?

_____

_____

12. How can a break-even analysis be used when planning a business?

_____

_____

_____

Crossword

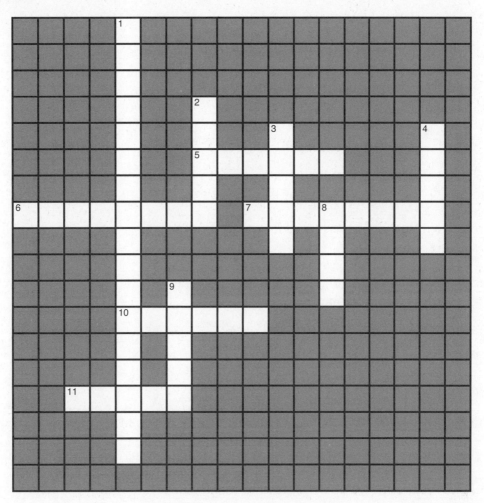

Use the clues below to solve the puzzle, which contains many vocabulary terms from Section 12.2.

Across

5. Type of statement that shows whether a business is making money or breaking even

6. When these, along with 11 ACROSS, are exactly equal to sales, a business breaks even

7. The break-even _____ examines how much of a product a business must sell to pay costs

10. What a statement shows if a business does better than break even

11. When these, along with 6 ACROSS, are exactly equal to sales, a business breaks even

Down

1. On an income statement, these are the costs associated with running a business (2 words)

2. Break-even _____ are the number of items a business must sell to pay its expenses

3. Break-even _____ occurs when 6 ACROSS and 11 ACROSS together are exactly equal to sales

4. The _____ profit of a business is used to pay operating expenses

8. What a statement shows if a business does less than break even

9. A business can sell units of a product or _____ of a service

STUDY GUIDE 12.2

Check Yourself

In the sentences below, fill in the blanks with the correct answer.

1. A break-even analysis is based on examination of data in the _____.

2. At the break-even point a business has neither a _____ nor
   a _____.

3. Net income is _____ at the break-even point.

4. A break-even analysis tells you how many units of a product (or hours of a service)
   you must _____ to pay all of the business' _____.

5. An entrepreneur whose business is taking a loss should _____ or eliminate
   expenese and/or find ways to _____ sales.

6. If a business sells fewer units than its number of break-even units, it
   will _____ money.

7. Subtracting the Cost of Goods Sold per Unit from the Selling _____ per
   Unit provides the Gross Profit per Unit.

Circle whether each statement is true or false.

8. True   False   At the break-even point a business has sold too little to pay its expenses.

9. True   False   When expenses equal sales, a business has neither a profit nor a loss.

10. True   False   A break-even analysis identifies the break-even point.

11. True   False   During July Matt's Hats must sell 300 hats to reach the break-even point.

12. True   False   Sales and expenses can change frequently.

13. True   False   Gross profit is used to pay operating expenses.

14. True   False   Revenue divided by gross profit per unit equals break-even units.

Extend Your Knowledge

New businesses typically bring in less money at first than they will need to cover
expenses. Successful new businesses manage to increase sales (and/or reduce expenses)
over their first few months or years in business to a point where sales do cover expenses.
This break-even point is an important goal for a newly started business. Goal setting,
in general, is considered a wise business strategy. Some entrepreneurs follow a SMART
approach to goal setting, where each letter in the acronym SMART describes the types
of goals that should be set. Using Internet resources learn about SMART goal setting
in business. Present a PowerPoint presentation to the class in which you share what you
have learned. Make sure the presentation is the length specified by the instructor.

STUDY GUIDE
Section 13.1

Start-Up Investment

Before You Begin

Think about the following question:

Can you start a business without borrowing money?

Answer: ☐ **Yes**   ☐ **No**

How much money does it take to get a business started?

_____

_____

_____

_____

_____

_____

Should an entrepreneur wait to start a business until he or she has saved up enough money to cover the start-up costs? Why or why not?

_____

_____

_____

_____

_____

Why might an entrepreneur borrow some money to help with start-up costs?

_____

_____

_____

_____

_____

Concepts Review

STUDY GUIDE 13.1

1. Explain why the start-up investment is a one-time sum.

   _____

   _____

   _____

2. Name the two components of a start-up investment.

   _____

   _____

   _____

3. How does an entrepreneur calculate the start-up expenditures for a new business?

   _____

   _____

   _____

4. List the two purposes for which cash reserves are set aside.

   _____

   _____

   _____

5. How much money should there be in an emergency fund?

   _____

   _____

   _____

6. How much should be in the reserve for fixed expenses?

   _____

   _____

   _____

   _____

7. Explain payback time.

_____

_____

_____

_____

8. What does it mean for an entrepreneur to "bootstrap"?

_____

_____

9. Name the two ways that entrepreneurs can begin their businesses by bootstrapping.

_____

_____

_____

10. What are the advantages and disadvantages of using personal savings to start a business?

_____

_____

_____

_____

_____

11. What are the advantages and disadvantages of using credit cards to fund the start-up expenditures of a business?

_____

_____

_____

_____

STUDY GUIDE 13.1

Crossword

Use the clues below to solve the puzzle, which contains many vocabulary terms from Section 13.1.

Across

1. Amount of time it takes a business to earn a profit after the initial investment

6. A new business should set aside a _____ for fixed costs, such as rent

7. One-time cost to get a new business going is a _____ investment

8. Using _____ is a strategy for funding a new business (2 words)

10. Raising money for a business

11. Another name for 5 DOWN (2 words)

Down

2. Starting a business by yourself, without any outside investment

3. Using _____ is a strategy for funding a new business (2 words)

4. Money a new business should set aside for unexpected expenses (2 words)

5. Investment funds to get a new business going (3 words)

9. Using 8 ACROSS for funding can damage your credit _____

Check Yourself

In the sentences below, fill in the blanks with the correct answer.

1. Start-up investment is also called _____
   or _____.

2. The start-up investment is calculated by adding together the start-up _____,
   the _____ fund, and the reserve for _____ expenses.

3. A business with a start-up investment of $12,000 and a net profit per month of $2,000 has
   a payback of _____.

4. Bootstrapping is possible if the amount you have to invest is _____ than the
   start-up investment.

5. If you use your personal savings to finance your business all the profit will belong
   to _____.

6. Keeping _____ balances on your credit cards can negatively affect your
   credit rating.

Circle whether each statement is true or false.

7. True   False   Entrepreneurs should calculate what their start-up expenditures will be.

8. True   False   Cash reserves is money that you spend on start-up equipment.

9. True   False   The start-up investment should be more than the start-up expenditures.

10. True   False   Payback is start-up investment divided by fixed expenses.

11. True   False   Bootstrapping means doing something completely on your own.

12. True   False   Bootstrapping is typically the most desirable way to start a business.

13. True   False   Using credit cards for your start-up investment is always a good idea.

Extend Your Knowledge

Although entrepreneurs may be tempted to use credit cards to pay for start-up expenditures, experts recommend against this practice. Most credit card companies charge compound interest rather than simple interest. Many people do not understand the difference between these two types of interest. Use Internet resources to learn about these concepts and how they apply to different kinds of debt, for example, bank loans and credit cards. Prepare a PowerPoint presentation for the class on simple and compound interest. Use examples to illustrate how the interest rate type affects the amount of money that must be paid back. Make sure your presentation is the length specified by the instructor, and be prepared to answer questions from your classmates.

STUDY GUIDE 13.1

STUDY GUIDE
Section 13.2

Obtaining Financing

Before You Begin

Think about the following question:

Would you borrow money from friends or family members to start a business?

Answer: ☐ **Yes**   ☐ **No**

If **Yes**, why would you borrow money from them?

_____

_____

_____

_____

If **No**, why would you not borrow money from them?

_____

_____

_____

_____

How would you feel if you borrowed money from family or friends to start a business and then the business failed? How do you think they would feel?

_____

_____

_____

_____

_____

Concepts Review

1. Name the three mains sources of debt financing.

   _____

2. How does a bank use a bank debt ratio to make loan decisions?

   _____

   _____

3. How does a credit union differ from a bank?

   _____

   _____

4. What are the advantages and risks associated with borrowing start-up capital from relatives and friends?

   _____

   _____

   _____

   _____

5. What is equity financing?

   _____

6. Name the three main sources of equity financing.

   _____

7. What is the primary difference between obtaining equity financing from friends or relatives and obtaining debt financing from them?

   _____

   _____

8. How are angels different from venture capital companies.

   _____

   _____

   _____

9. What are the advantages and disadvantages of obtaining equity financing from a business partner?

_____

_____

_____

_____

10. List four specialized sources of financing for business start-ups.

_____

_____

11. How can debt financing and equity financing affect a business's balance sheet?

_____

_____

12. About what rate of return does a venture capitalist expect on an investment?

_____

13. A venture capitalist invests $5 million for a 25% equity. What is the company's value?

_____

14. A venture capitalist has 40% equity in a company with an estimated value of $10 million. How much is the venture capitalist's share worth?

_____

15. A venture capitalist invested $10,000. When the company went public, she received 600 shares of stock, which she sold at $100 per share. What was her gross profit?

_____

16. Using the same information, find her ROI.

_____

17. What is the ROI on an investment of $160,000 that returns $80,000 in profits?

_____

Crossword

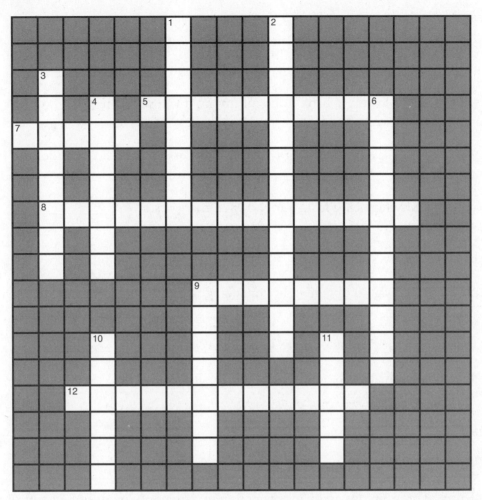

Use the clues below to solve the puzzle, which contains many vocabulary terms from Section 13.2.

Across

5. Property or assets you pledge to a lender to secure a loan

7. Investor who is interested in helping start-up businesses

8. Selling shares of ownership in a business to raise money (2 words)

9. Individual, such as a relative or friend, who guarantees loan payments to a lender

12. Source for 2 DOWN (2 words)

Down

1. What the "M" of "MESBIC" stands for

2. Borrowing additional money to fund a start-up business (2 words)

3. If you use 11 DOWN for funds, a _____ ratio shows your monthly income compared to what you borrowed (2 words)

4. With 9 DOWN, money invested in a potentially profitable business by a company that invests in start-ups

6. Desirable type of loan (2 words)

9. See 4 DOWN

10. System of trading items between businesses

11. Source for 2 DOWN

STUDY GUIDE 13.2

Check Yourself

In the sentences below, fill in the blanks with the correct answer.

1. A bank debt ratio is calculated by dividing monthly debt payments by monthly _____ and then multiplying by _____.

2. If you fail to repay a loan to a bank or credit union, it can seize the _____ that you pledged to secure the loan.

3. Before deciding to use debt financing to start a business you should consider the monthly payments and the _____ rate on the loan.

4. If you obtain equity financing from a friend then that person will _____ a part of your business.

5. Venture capitalists invest in less than _____ of the businesses they consider.

6. The most common way to obtain equity financing is to split ownership of the business with a _____.

7. Barter financing is the trading of items or services between _____.

8. Using debt financing affects the balance sheet by increasing the business's _____.

Circle whether each statement is true or false.

9. True   False   Borrowing money to start up a business is called equity financing.

10. True   False   Credit unions and banks may require someone to co-sign a loan for you.

11. True   False   If you use equity financing you will completely control your business.

12. True   False   Debt financing means you borrow money that has to be paid back.

13. True   False   Angels and venture capitalists are not interested in making a profit.

14. True   False   SBICs and MSBICs often charge higher interest rates than banks.

15. True   False   Using equity financing changes the owner's equity on the balance sheet.

16. True   False   Your customers might be willing to invest in your business.

Extend Your Knowledge

Business incubators are a little-known source of help for entrepreneurial start-ups. Research business incubators on the Internet and write a paper explaining how they can help new businesses obtain financing and facilities. Explain the difference between non-profit incubators and for-profit incubators. Make sure your paper is the length specified by the instructor.

STUDY GUIDE
Section 14.1

Recordkeeping

Before You Begin

Think about the following question:

Do you keep records of your purchases?

Answer: ☐ Yes   ☐ No

If **Yes**, why do you keep records of your purchases?

_____

_____

_____

_____

_____

_____

If **No**, why don't you keep records of your purchases?

_____

_____

_____

_____

_____

_____

Why would a business owner keep records of his or her business purchases?

_____

_____

_____

_____

_____

_____

Concepts Review

1. Describe the benefits of having a checking account.

_____

_____

_____

_____

2. What are the three main steps involved in reconciling your checkbook with your monthly bank statement?

_____

_____

_____

_____

_____

3. How are receipts useful in recordkeeping?

_____

_____

_____

_____

4. What is the difference between a purchase order and a sales invoice?

_____

_____

_____

_____

5. Why is it important to keep good business records?

_____

_____

6. What are the five steps in a simple double-entry accounting system?

_____

_____

_____

_____

_____

_____

_____

7. What are the two approaches for recording transactions and what kind of systems use each one?

_____

_____

8. Explain duality.

_____

_____

_____

_____

_____

9. What are the advantages of computerized accounting systems?

_____

_____

10. Give an advantage and disadvantage of using an accountant or bookkeeper to maintain your books.

_____

_____

_____

STUDY GUIDE 14.1

Crossword

Use the clues below to solve the puzzle, which contains many vocabulary terms from Section 14.1.

Across

1. With 10 ACROSS, what "PO" means

7. Accountant who checks the books of a company

9. Accounting system in which every business activity affects at least two accounts (2 words)

10. With 1 ACROSS, what "PO" means

11. Detailed written proof of purchase

12. What the "F" in "FDIC" stands for

13. Type of bank account in which you deposit money

Down

2. The process of balancing a checkbook is bank _____

3. Crime of stealing money from an employer

4. An original record, such as a cancelled check, is an example of this (2 words)

5. Type of card you can use to remove money from a checking account

6. Person to whom you write a check

8. Accounting term for any payment or income received

Name _____Class_____Date _____

Check Yourself

In the sentences below, fill in the blanks with the correct answer.

1. Cancelled checks may be sent to you, or you might have access to them at the bank or through the bank's _____.

2. A purchase order should clearly state what it is you want to _____.

3. The single-column, database method requires that any change in the left side of the equation Assets = Liabilities + Owner's Equity must _____ a change on the right side.

4. In the double-column method the _____ must always equal the _____ when you record a transaction.

5. At the end of each reporting period the account balances should be _____ and transferred to the financial statements.

6. Accounting software packages for small business are often called general _____ programs.

7. Accounting controls allow a business owner more control over financial operations and also help prevent _____ by hired accountants or bookkeepers.

Circle whether each statement is true or false.

8. True   False   Cancelled checks provide proof that payees received money from you.

9. True   False   You should save the receipts from your ATM and debit card transactions.

10. True   False   When you purchase supplies you should print a receipt for the supplier.

11. True   False   A sales invoice is another name for a purchase order.

12. True   False   Asset increases are recorded on the debit side in a double-column system.

13. True   False   Software accounting systems prepare financial statements automatically.

14. True   False   It doesn't cost any money to hire an accountant or bookkeeper.

Extend Your Knowledge

One of the challenges of operating a business is organizing and storing paper financial records, such as receipts, bank statements, purchase orders, sales invoices, bills, etc. Use the Internet to research options for organizing and storing these records. Write a paper summarizing your recommendations for a new small business owner. Make sure your paper is the length specified by the instructor.

STUDY GUIDE 14.1

STUDY GUIDE
Section 14.2

Accounting Systems

Before You Begin

Think about the following question:

As an entrepreneur, would you use a manual accounting system or a computerized accounting system for your business?

_____

When working with numbers do you prefer to use a pencil and paper or would you rather use a computer? Why?

_____

_____

_____

_____

Do you prefer using paper or the computer for your written communications and expressions (letters, stories, poems, diaries, etc.)? Why?

_____

_____

_____

_____

As an entrepreneur, would you use a manual (paper-based) accounting system or a computerized accounting system for your business? Why?

_____

_____

_____

_____

Concepts Review

1. Explain why an accounting worksheet is "real-time."

   _____

   _____

   _____

   _____

2. Give some tips for keeping a handwritten (manual) accounting worksheet.

   _____

   _____

   _____

   _____

3. Give the accounting equation and explain how the accounting worksheet template in Figure 14-5 is organized according to the accounting equation.

   _____

   _____

   _____

   _____

4. What is the purpose of the Pacioli check column on the accounting worksheet?

   _____

   _____

   _____

   _____

5. Explain how Jean's current cash account changed from $2,000 to $1,400 on August 2.

   _____

   _____

   _____

   _____

STUDY GUIDE 14.2

6. Which accounts change when Jean purchases T-shirts?

_____

_____

7. Which accounts change when Jean sells T-shirts?

_____

_____

8. List all the expense accounts listed on Jean's accounting worksheet.

_____

_____

9. How are data in rows 10 and 29 on the accounting worksheet used in a balance sheet.

_____

_____

_____

_____

_____

_____

10. Explain how account codes assist you in preparing an income statement.

_____

_____

_____

_____

11. Name the three types of business activities that are included on the statement of cash flows.

_____

_____

_____

Crossword

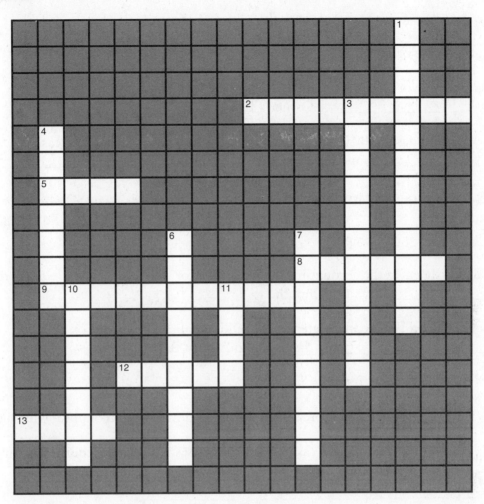

Use the clues below to solve the puzzle, which contains many vocabulary terms from Section 14.2.

Across

2. Type of business activity that involves buying assets that will last more than one year

5. Worksheets are made up of columns and _____

8. A(n) _____ transaction is one that is written in an accounting worksheet

9. What "A/C" stands for on a worksheet (2 words)

12. Name of software used to create worksheets

13. Connect numbers from one part of an electronic worksheet to another

Down

1. Worksheet column that ensures the accounting equation balances after each transaction (2 words)

3. Another name for a worksheet

4. In an electronic worksheet, "=sum(d1:d10)" is an example of this

6. Type of business activity that would include applying cash for startup equity

7. Type of basic, day-to-day business activity

10. In an electronic worksheet, you can add a note to a specific data entry by inserting this

11. In an electronic worksheet, you enter data into this structure

Name _____ Class _____ Date _____

Check Yourself

In the sentences below, fill in the blanks with the correct answer.

1. An accounting worksheet uses the _____-column approach.

2. An accounting worksheet is organized according to the accounting equation:
   Assets = _____ + Owner's Equity.

3. When Jean purchased 400 T-shirts on August 15 her cash account decreased
   by _____ and her inventory account increased by _____.

4. A completed accounting worksheet includes an _____ statement, a beginning
   and ending _____ sheet, a statement of _____ flows, and
   an _____ report.

5. The balance sheets in the accounting worksheet are for the _____ day and
   _____ day of the month.

6. The net profit on the income statement should equal the net profit on
   the _____ that is dated August 31.

Circle whether each statement is true or false.

7. True   False   A computerized spreadsheet is one option for an accounting worksheet.

8. True   False   An increase to the cash account increases the owner's equity account.

9. True   False   The computer that Jean bought is a COGS expense.

10. True   False   The balance sheets must be prepared before the income statement.

11. True   False   In every balance sheet the total assets must equal the total liabilities.

12. True   False   A statement of cash flows shows the cash balance at the end of the month.

13. True   False   In an accounting spreadsheet you can add comments to cells.

Extend Your Knowledge

One of the first steps in most accounting systems is creating a chart of accounts
and assigning codes to the accounts. The example in this section for Jean Waverly's
T-Shirts uses letters combined with 1-digit numerical codes, for example, R1 or FE3.
Use Internet resources to learn about different code systems that are commonly
recommended and used. Give a PowerPoint presentation to the class about what you
have learned. Include examples from several different account-code systems. Make sure
your presentation is the length specified by the instructor.

STUDY GUIDE
Section 15.1

Hiring Decisions

Before You Begin

Think about the following question:

What task would you pay someone else to do for you?

_____

Why do you not want to perform that task yourself?

_____

_____

_____

_____

How would it benefit you if someone performed that task for you for free?

_____

_____

_____

_____

How much would you be willing to pay someone to do that task for you?

_____

_____

_____

_____

Concepts Review

1. Name some advantages to a business owner of having employees.

    _____

    _____

    _____

    _____

2. Name some disadvantages to a business owner of having employees.

    _____

    _____

    _____

    _____

    _____

3. What are six questions an entrepreneur should consider before hiring employees?

    _____

    _____

    _____

    _____

    _____

4. What is an organizational structure?

    _____

    _____

5. List the three types of traditional organizational business structures.

    _____

    _____

6. Describe some new trends in organizational structures.

_____

_____

_____

_____

7. What should be listed in a job description in order to attract only qualified applicants?

_____

_____

_____

_____

8. List the three factors that employers must consider in determining the amount of employee compensation to offer.

_____

_____

_____

9. Name some sources for locating potential job candidates.

_____

_____

_____

10. What are some things a potential employer should look for in a resume?

_____

_____

_____

_____

11. Why do some businesses hire outside specialists?

_____

_____

Crossword

Use the clues below to solve the puzzle, which contains many vocabulary terms from Section 15.1.

Across

3. With 5 DOWN, a system for dividing work, authority, and responsibility in a company

7. What an employee receives in exchange for working

9. Weekly, bimonthly, or monthly payment paid to an employee

11. With 4 DOWN, the people who work in a business

12. Explanation of a position's purpose, tasks, and responsibilities (2 words)

13. Find and hire qualified candidates for a job

14. _____ organization shows the direct chain of command of personnel who are directly involved in a business's main occupation

Down

1. Written summary of work experience, education, and skills

2. Health insurance, paid vacation, and sick days are examples of these

4. With 11 ACROSS, the people who work in a business

5. With 3 ACROSS, a system for dividing work, authority, and responsibility in a company

6. Payment to employees per hour worked or piece of work completed

8. College _____ offices connect employers to job-seeking students

10. _____ organization gathers employees from more than one department to work as a team on a specific goal

Name _____ Class_____ Date _____

Check Yourself

In the sentences below, fill in the blanks with the correct answer.

1. In order to deduct taxes from an employee's paychecks an employer must first file a _____ Form and a _____ Form with the IRS.

2. In a traditional line-organization structure the business owner is at the _____ level.

3. Employee compensation includes both money and _____.

4. Applications and _____ are documents that summarize information for employers about job seekers.

5. An employer should write a job _____ for each position that needs filling.

6. When hiring an outside specialist a business owner should ask candidates for _____ from their other clients.

7. A company that locates and recommends potential employees to an employer is called a _____ agency.

8. Before interviewing job applicants you should make a list of _____ you plan to ask them.

Circle whether each statement is true or false.

9. True   False   Employees may supply skills and qualities the entrepreneur does not have.

10. True   False   Employees mean less paperwork and expense for the business owner.

11. True   False   Most businesses never change their organizational structure.

12. True   False   A project organization structure ends once the project goal is reached.

13. True   False   Choosing employees wisely is critical to a small business.

14. True   False   Health insurance and paid vacation are examples of benefits.

15. True   False   Outside specialists are typically hired to be permanent employees.

16. True   False   A job description is also called a resume.

Extend Your Knowledge

Use the Internet to learn useful tips for evaluating resumes. Write a paper summarizing what you have learned. Include a checklist of at least ten items, qualities, or characteristics that an employer should look for when reviewing a resume from a job seeker. Make sure your paper is the length specified by the instructor.

Name _____ Class _____ Date _____

Before You Begin

Think about the following question:

Are you motivated by school?

Answer: ☐ **Yes** ☐ **No**

If **Yes**, what are the factors about school that motivate you?

_____

_____

_____

_____

_____

If **No**, why aren't you motivated by school?

_____

_____

_____

_____

_____

What would it take to get you motivated or make you more motivated by school?

_____

_____

_____

_____

_____

Concepts Review

1. Explain why even qualified job candidates need employee training and development after they are hired.

   _____

   _____

   _____

   _____

   _____

2. Define in-house training and give two examples of it.

   _____

   _____

   _____

   _____

3. Name five qualities that a mentor should have.

   _____

   _____

   _____

   _____

4. List four options for training and development in settings outside of the business location.

   _____

   _____

5. Name some guidelines that employers should follow regarding performance-based rewards.

   _____

   _____

   _____

   _____

   _____

6. List some ways that employers can provide flexible work arrangements for employees.

_____

_____

_____

_____

7. Name two techniques that an employer can use to delegate more responsibility to employees.

_____

_____

8. List some ways that employers can create a positive environment in the workplace.

_____

_____

_____

_____

_____

9. Name the two goals of performance evaluations.

_____

_____

10. What are the benefits of promoting an existing employee when a higher-level job becomes available.

_____

_____

_____

_____

11. What should an employer do when he or she is considering firing an employee?

_____

_____

_____

Crossword

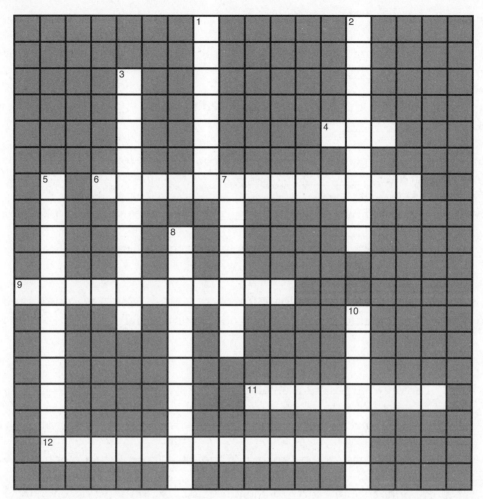

Use the clues below to solve the puzzle, which contains many vocabulary terms from Section 15.2.

Across

4. With 2 DOWN, process of learning by watching an employee perform over a period of time

6. Certification by a professional group that an individual has certain skills

9. Process of gradually integrating an employee into a workplace

11. Work schedule that allows employees to start or finish an hour earlier or later than others

12. Working from a location other than the business site

Down

1. To _____ an employee is to offer a higher-level, better-paying job

2. With 4 ACROSS, process of learning by watching an employee perform over a period of time

3. Job _____ means increasing the depth or involvement of a position

5. Job _____ means adding responsibilities to a position

7. To _____ an employee is to fire that individual

8. Performance _____ is a regular employee review

10. Person who receives guidance in a mentoring relationship

STUDY GUIDE 15.2

Check Yourself

In the sentences below, fill in the blanks with the correct answer.

1. The process of introducing a new employee to other workers and giving him or her a tour of the workplace is called _____.

2. Milton Hershey believed that people are motivated to work _____ when they feel _____.

3. The purpose of job enlargement is not to provide more work for an employee to do, but to give him or her greater _____.

4. Employees are motivated by a _____ atmosphere in the workplace.

5. When you do performance evaluations you help your employees improve their _____ and improve your workplace.

6. Employers that must dismiss an employee for _____ reasons should make clear to the employee that losing the job was not his or her fault.

Circle whether each statement is true or false.

7. True   False   The only purpose of training is to improve employee skills.

8. True   False   It may be necessary to fire an unproductive or troublesome employee.

9. True   False   A protégé has greater experience and knowledge than a mentor.

10. True   False   A conference or expo may include classes, workshops, or seminars.

11. True   False   All motivational techniques are expensive.

12. True   False   Employees do not value flexibility in their work schedules.

13. True   False   To delegate responsibility means to give employees more responsibilities.

14. True   False   A performance evaluation is typically done through a one-to-one meeting.

Extend Your Knowledge

Some business magazines and associations occasionally conduct informal surveys to determine which companies are most popular with their employees. The "winning" companies are often promoted as "the best companies to work for." Use the Internet to learn and read about recent surveys on this topic. Focus on the characteristics that employees named as the reasons they felt their company was a great place to work. Present your findings to the class in an oral presentation. Make sure your presentation is the length specified by the instructor.

STUDY GUIDE
Section 16.1

Legal Issues

Before You Begin

Think about the following question:

Have you ever considered copying songs from a CD onto a computer?

Answer: ☐ **Yes** ☐ **No**

If **Yes**, do you see anything wrong with copying songs from a CD onto your computer and then sharing those song files with your friends? Explain.

_____

_____

_____

_____

If **No**, do you worry that copying songs from a CD onto your computer could be illegal? Explain.

_____

_____

_____

_____

Why do you think recording artists don't want people to copy songs from CDs and then share the song files with others?

_____

_____

_____

_____

_____

Concepts Review

1. What is intellectual property?

   _____

   _____

2. What is a copyright, when does it come into existence, and how long does it last?

   _____

   _____

   _____

   _____

3. When can you obtain a patent?

   _____

   _____

   _____

4. If you invent a new software program, how should you protect it? What protection should you try to obtain if you invent a new mechanical device?

   _____

   _____

5. Name the three general types of patents granted by the U.S. Patent and Trademark Office and list what each type covers.

   _____

   _____

   _____

6. What are the five categories of inventions covered by utility patents?

   _____

   _____

   _____

Name _____ Class_____ Date _____

7. Name the three conditions that an invention must meet in order to be patented.

_____

_____

8. What are the benefits of registering a trademark or service mark?

_____

_____

_____

_____

9. List the four factors under the Uniform Trade Secrets Act that determine whether or not information qualifies as a trade secret.

_____

_____

_____

10. Name some common types of contracts used in business.

_____

_____

11. Name the three conditions that make a contract valid, or legally enforceable.

_____

_____

12. Create a sample contract between you and a wholesaler for business supplies.

_____

_____

_____

_____

_____

_____

Crossword

Use the clues below to solve the puzzle, which contains many vocabulary terms from Section 16.1.

Across

5. Events or circumstances that must occur for a contract to be binding

7. Written contract for temporary use of a property

10. Information that a business keeps confidential to gain advantage over competitors (2 words)

11. Things that have value but are not material goods

12. Type of agreement that binds parties to secrecy

13. This provides rights to use intellectual property

Down

1. Failure to carry out the conditions of a contract is a _____ of contract

2. Legally, being _____ means being capable of understanding the terms of a contract

3. The benefit each party provides to the other in a mutual exchange

4. Violation of the rights provided by a copyright

6. Payment that a guilty party must pay to reimburse the injured party for loss

8. "SM" next to a company name indicates this (2 words)

9. A work based on one or more existing works

Check Yourself

In the sentences below, fill in the blanks with the correct answer.

1. U.S. law gives creators an exclusive right to their creative works, but only for limited _____ periods.

2. Although a verbal contract can be a valid contract, it is better for both parties if a contract is in _____.

3. Infringing on a registered copyright is a federal _____.

4. A patent grants the exclusive right to make, use, or sell the work for _____ years from the date on which the patent is filed.

5. A common remedy sought by parties who believe that they have been hurt by copyright or patent infringement is _____.

6. The most numerous patents issued are_____ patents.

7. When people refer to a product by its brand name, they are mentioning its _____ or _____.

Circle whether each statement is true or false.

8. True   False   The importance of creativity was recognized in the U.S. Constitution.

9. True   False   Intellectual property law covers almost any kind of creation.

10. True   False   A copyright cannot be transferred to someone else.

11. True   False   Obtaining a patent is easy and inexpensive.

12. True   False   A child can legally enter into a contract with someone else.

13. True   False   The purpose of a nondisclosure agreement is to keep something secret.

14. True   False   Damages are payments that guilty contract breakers may have to pay.

15. True   False   A trademark can include offensive or stereotypical images.

Extend Your Knowledge

Use the Internet to learn about knock-offs and counterfeit goods. In what countries are most of these goods purchased and sold? How are these goods harmful to legitimate businesses? How are they harmful to society in general? Present your findings to the class in an oral presentation. Make sure your presentation is the length specified by the instructor.

STUDY GUIDE
Section 16.2

Insurance

Before You Begin

Think about the following question:

Can you tolerate risk?

Answer: ☐ **Yes** ☐ **No**

If **Yes**, name the types of risk you are willing to take—for example, health, safety, financial, etc., and how much risk you can handle.

_____

_____

_____

_____

_____

If **No**, explain why you avoid taking risks.

_____

_____

_____

_____

_____

_____

Are some risks bad and other risks good? Explain.

_____

_____

_____

_____

_____

Concepts Review

1. What is the difference between speculative risk and pure risk, and how are they managed differently?

_____

_____

_____

_____

2. Describe an insurance policy.

_____

_____

_____

_____

3. What items are covered by a basic property insurance policy?

_____

_____

_____

4. List the three most common types of liability insurance and 2 types that are growing in popularity.

_____

_____

_____

_____

5. What types of payouts are possible under workers' compensation insurance?

_____

_____

6. Name two possible sources for information and advice about choosing an insurance agent.

_____

_____

7. What is a rider?

_____

_____

8. List some options for securing physical property.

_____

_____

_____

_____

_____

9. Name some ways that businesses can safeguard information.

_____

_____

_____

_____

_____

10. List some ways that businesses can try to prevent accidents, injury, and crime in the workplace.

_____

_____

_____

_____

_____

_____

Crossword

Use the clues below to solve the puzzle, which contains many vocabulary terms from Section 16.2.

Across

3. Amount of money an insured person or business pays for coverage

6. Hurricanes are classified as this type of risk

8. Written contract between an insurance company and the person that bought the insurance

10. Risk that holds the possibility of either gain or loss

11. With 5 DOWN, type of insurance that covers losses to employees due to job-related injury

13. Type of insurance that provides protection if a business's action injures another party

14. Insurance companies predict risk by using the law of _____ (2 words)

Down

1. Type of insurance that protects a business's possessions

2. Study of designing environments to fit the people using them

4. Purchasing business insurance is an example of risk _____

5. With 11 ACROSS, type of insurance that covers losses to employees due to job-related injury

7. Amendment that changes the benefits or conditions of insurance coverage

9. The actual worth for which a business's possessions can be insured (2 words)

12. Risk that holds the chance of loss with no gain

Check Yourself

In the sentences below, fill in the blanks with the correct answer.

1. Insurance companies are experts at managing _____.

2. Starting a business is a speculative risk, because there is the possibility of either _____ or _____.

3. Business owners who rent property should purchase _____ insurance.

4. General liability insurance covers injuries or damages due to employee _____ at work.

5. Although workers' compensation insurance is required in every state, in some states, businesses with _____ or fewer employees are exempt.

6. An exclusive insurance agent works for _____ insurance company, while an _____ insurance agent represents several insurance companies.

7. Practicing risk reduction and prevention tends to _____ the cost of insurance premiums.

Circle whether the statements are true or false.

8. True   False   One component of managing risk is preparing for the worst.

9. True   False   To manage pure risk means to avoid it or reduce it.

10. True   False   Experts recommend that property be insured for its cash value.

11. True   False   An insurance policy typically covers the entire amount of a loss.

12. True   False   Error and omission insurance is a type of product liability insurance.

13. True   False   Your business should have insurance coverage before it even opens.

14. True   False   Providing a safe workplace is a legal and ethical responsibility.

15. True   False   A kitchen fire in a restaurant is a speculative risk.

Extend Your Knowledge

Workers' compensation insurance is required by state law in every state. However, specific requirements do vary between states. Use the Internet to research the workers' compensation insurance program in your state. Write a paper presenting an overview of the program. Be sure to note if businesses of a certain size or type of if certain types of workers are exempt from the state program requirements. Are there other types of workers' compensation programs? Make sure your paper is the length specified by the instructor.

Name _____ Class _____ Date _____

Taxes & Your Business

Before You Begin

Think about the following question:

Do you personally pay taxes?

Answer: ☐ Yes   ☐ No

If you get a paycheck, what kinds of taxes are deducted from it?

_____

_____

_____

_____

_____

When you purchase goods at the store, what kinds of taxes are added to the purchase price?

_____

_____

_____

_____

_____

What kinds of taxes do you think business owners pay?

_____

_____

_____

_____

_____

Name _____ Class_____ Date _____

Concepts Review

1. List the broad types of public services that are provided by the government.

   _____

   _____

   _____

   _____

2. Name some federal programs and agencies that provide social services.

   _____

   _____

   _____

3. List some benefits to the American people of taxes spent on the armed forces.

   _____

   _____

   _____

   _____

   _____

4. Name some ways in which businesses benefit from government programs.

   _____

   _____

   _____

   _____

5. Describe FICA taxes and who pays them.

   _____

   _____

   _____

   _____

6. Describe the FUTA tax and who pays it.

_____

_____

_____

_____

7. What are the two main types of consumption taxes.

_____

_____

8. Define estimated taxes and note who pays them and when.

_____

_____

_____

_____

9. What kinds of business property may be subject to property taxes?

_____

_____

_____

_____

_____

10. List some common business expenses that can be tax deductions.

_____

_____

_____

_____

_____

_____

Crossword

Use the clues below to solve the puzzle, which contains many vocabulary terms from Section 17.1.

Across

1. Tax _____ is a dollar-for-dollar reduction in taxes owed

5. Tax _____ is using legal strategies to reduce one's tax liability

6. With 11 DOWN, area in which businesses receive economic incentives to develop

9. Financial aid from the government to support an industry or public service

10. The "F" in FICA

12. The most common type of consumption tax

13. Type of sales made within the state where the company is physically located

14. Tax _____ is the illegal avoidance of paying taxes

Down

2. Tax on a specific product or commercial activity

3. Type of 8 DOWN that includes business transportation, meals, and lodging

4. System of organizations and services that society needs to function

7. Type of taxes FICA refers to

8. Item or expense subtracted from gross income in a tax return

10. The "F" in "TIF"

11. With 6 ACROSS, area in which businesses receive economic incentives to develop

Check Yourself

In the sentences below, fill in the blanks with the correct answer.

1. Social services account for almost _____ of all federal government spending.

2. Social Security provides benefits for _____ workers, dependents of _____ workers, and workers who have _____ and their dependents.

3. Approximately _____ of the federal government's budget provides for the nation's armed forces.

4. Although both employers and workers pay FICA taxes, the _____ is responsible for calculating and sending the payments to the IRS.

5. Expenses that are considered "_____ and _____" for operating a business are typically tax-deductible.

6. A tax deduction lowers your taxable _____, while a tax credit lowers the _____ itself.

7. One business expense commonly taken as a tax deduction by producers and wholesalers is their costs of goods _____.

Circle whether each statement is true or false.

8. True   False   Taxes buy government services.

9. True   False   An employer matches the FICA payments of his or her employees.

10. True   False   Deductions increase the amount of tax you must pay.

11. True   False   Employee-paid payroll taxes are withheld from each paycheck.

12. True   False   Property tax rates are set by the federal government.

13. True   False   Taxes fund public schools, city buses, and law enforcement.

14. True   False   The federal government charges a sales tax on all purchases.

Extend Your Knowledge

Self-employed people do not pay a FICA tax, but a similar tax under the Self Employment Contribution Act (SECA) that helps fund the Social Security and Medicare programs. Use the Internet to learn about the SECA tax and how it is calculated. Present a PowerPoint presentation to the class on this topic. Use specific examples, and show the mathematical calculations that are necessary to figure the tax. Make sure the presentation is the length specified by the instructor.

STUDY GUIDE
Section 17.2

Government Regulations

Before You Begin

Think about the following question:

Would you be able to play a sport that had no rules?

Answer: ☐ **Yes** ☐ **No**

How do rules help keep a game fair for all competitors?

_____

_____

_____

_____

_____

Why are sports rules enforced during a game by somebody other than the contestants?

_____

_____

_____

_____

_____

Do rules make it easier or harder to win at a sport? Explain.

_____

_____

_____

_____

_____

Concepts Review

1. Why did the government begin to exert control over American businesses in the 1800s?

_____

_____

_____

_____

2. List the requirements of five OSHA regulations that apply to many businesses.

_____

_____

_____

_____

_____

_____

_____

_____

3. Describe the laws that require a minimum wage and impose other requirements related to work hours and pay for some workers.

_____

_____

_____

_____

4. Name the government laws that protect employees against discrimination, and the general types of discrimination that are prohibited.

_____

_____

_____

STUDY GUIDE 17.2

5. List the federal government agencies that handle regulation of packaging, labeling, and product safety.

_____

_____

_____

6. What three characteristics does the FTC require for advertisements?

_____

_____

7. What is the difference between a license and a permit?

_____

_____

_____

_____

8. What types of requirements are typically included in zoning laws?

_____

_____

_____

_____

9. Name the agency that sets environmental regulations at the federal level.

_____

10. Describe three exceptions from federal laws for small businesses.

_____

_____

_____

_____

_____

Crossword

Use the clues below to solve the puzzle, which contains many vocabulary terms from Section 17.2.

Across

1. Situation where a single supplier is a market's only provider of a certain product

3. What the "S" in "OSHA" stands for

4. The Fair Labor _____ Act is a fair-treatment law that protects workers' hours and wages

8. Notice for customers to return a product that poses health risks

10. These laws help ensure that businesses are good neighbors in the community

11. _____ products contain harmful substances or were modified to mask poor quality

12. Type of law that forbids anticompetitive mergers and business practices

13. Price _____ is when competing companies agree to set the cost of goods or services

Down

2. Legal document that allows a business to take a specific action, such as building a house

3. Amount of money given to employees when terminated for reasons other than performance (2 words)

5. Price _____ is charging competing buyers different prices for the same product

6. What the "E" in "EPA" stands for

7. What the "P" in "EPA" stands for

9. Government-issued legal document that allows a business to provide a product or service

STUDY GUIDE 17.2

Check Yourself

In the sentences below, fill in the blanks with the correct answer.

1. Not only has the federal government attempted to control industry, but _____ have often passed their own laws.

2. The Equal Employment _____ Commission (EEOC) enforces laws that promote a level playing field in the workplace.

3. The Americans with Disabilities Act requires employers to provide reasonable accommodations to make the workplace and job duties more _____ for qualified workers with disabilities.

4. The Fair Packaging and _____ Act requires all product packaging identify the item, its manufacturer, and the quantity of the item, either in weight or number.

5. The U.S. Consumer Product Safety Commission sets product safety standards for about _____ consumer goods.

6. The Clean Water Act may require a business to get a permit to discharge _____.

7. Small Business Advisory Review Panels have been set up by _____ to hear business owners' input on developing safety standards.

Circle whether each statement is true or false.

8. True   False   Some entrepreneurs feel that regulation is an obstacle to business growth.

9. True   False   The FDA and the USDA allow the sale of adulterated products.

10. True   False   OSHA enforces its rules through workplace inspections.

11. True   False   Antitrust laws are local ordinances that enforce zoning.

12. True   False   Employers must create an atmosphere of tolerance and respect at work.

13. True   False   Small businesses are exempted from all government regulations.

14. True   False   The FTC enforces truth-in-advertising laws.

15. True   False   There is no punishment for violating environmental laws.

Extend Your Knowledge

Use Internet resources to research the EEOC. How was it created? What is its purpose? What laws does it enforce? What types of discrimination does it investigate? How many discrimination claims does it investigate each year? Write a paper presenting your findings. Make sure the paper is the length specified by the instructor.

STUDY GUIDE
Section 18.1

How to Manage a Business

Before You Begin

Think about the following question:

Are you a leader?

Answer: ☐ Yes   ☐ No

If **Yes**, what qualities do you have that make you a leader?

_____

_____

_____

_____

_____

If **No**, why do you not consider yourself a leader?

_____

_____

_____

_____

_____

Why are people willing to follow a good leader?

_____

_____

_____

_____

_____

Concepts Review

1. What is the purpose of management?

_____

_____

_____

2. List the four general management functions.

_____

_____

3. Describe the three types of plans used in business management.

_____

_____

_____

_____

_____

_____

_____

_____

4. List the resources that should be organized within a business.

_____

_____

_____

5. Name some good interpersonal skills that a manager should have.

_____

_____

_____

6. List and briefly describe the three basic leadership styles.

_____

_____

_____

_____

_____

_____

_____

7. Name some of the components of a business for which performance standards can be set.

_____

_____

_____

8. What is a quality control program?

_____

_____

_____

9. What types of circumstance affect workplace climate?

_____

_____

_____

10. List some of the items and actions through which a business builds it company image.

_____

_____

_____

_____

_____

_____

Crossword

[Crossword puzzle grid with numbered squares 1–13]

Use the clues below to solve the puzzle, which contains many vocabulary terms from Section 18.1.

Across

5. Process of arranging and coordinating resources and tasks to achieve goals

7. Leadership style used when employees are told what to do without seeking their advice

9. Process of setting performance standards, measuring performance, and taking any needed corrective action

11. Type of plan that lays out a broad course of action to achieve a long-term goal

12. Type of skills used by people as they interact with others

13. Type of plan that details everyday activities for achieving short-range goals

Down

1. Leadership style used when employees are given freedom to decide what to do

2. Skillful use and coordination of a business's resources to achieve particular goals

3. Leadership style used when employees are asked for input about what to do

4. Program used to ensure that products or services meet specific standards (2 words)

6. Process of leading, influencing, and motivating employees to achieve goals

8. Type of plan that outlines major steps for carrying out a long-term plan and includes target dates

10. Process of setting goals and deciding how and when to accomplish them

Name _____ Class_____ Date _____

Check Yourself

In the sentences below, fill in the blanks with the correct answer.

1. One of the goals of management is to maximize _____ while minimizing _____.

2. A plan is a systematic process for achieving a specific _____.

3. Managers create organization charts that outline the chains of _____ within the business.

4. The ultimate goal of directing people is _____ building.

5. A group of well-organized people with a solid plan will not be successful without good _____.

6. Performance standards should be _____ and specific.

7. Companies build their image every time they interact with the _____.

8. A good company image contributes to a _____ workplace climate.

Circle whether the statements are true or false.

9. True   False   A manager should be a creative problem solver.

10. True   False   A strategic plan is a short-term plan covering just a few months.

11. True   False   Organizing creates structure.

12. True   False   A good manager is always a good leader.

13. True   False   New employees are typically led using a democratic leadership style.

14. True   False   Good leaders adjust their leadership style depending on the situation.

15. True   False   Most business tasks are accomplished by machines rather than people.

16. True   False   Managers play a major role in shaping the workplace climate.

Extend Your Knowledge

Use Internet resources to learn about the basic skills that people should have to be good managers and leaders. Do you believe that people are born with these skills? Do you believe that people can learn these skills in school or on the job? Present an oral presentation to the class in which you discuss the skills, why they are important, and your opinions about whether people are born with them and/or learn them. Make sure the presentation is the length specified by the instructor.

STUDY GUIDE 18.2

STUDY GUIDE
Section 18.2

Managing Expenses, Credit, & Cash Flow

Before You Begin

Think about the following question:

Which is better: "Buy now, pay now" or "Buy now, pay later"?

_____

What, if any, are the advantages of "buy now, pay now"?

_____

_____

_____

_____

What, if any, are the disadvantages of "buy now, pay now"?

_____

_____

_____

_____

What, if any, are the advantages of "buy now, pay later"?

_____

_____

_____

_____

What, if any, are the disadvantages of "buy now, pay later"?

_____

_____

_____

_____

Concepts Review

1. Describe the specific procedures that many businesses use when deciding whether or not to grant credit to an applicant.

   _____

   _____

   _____

   _____

   _____

2. Describe the actions that a creditor takes to make sure a debt is paid.

   _____

   _____

   _____

   _____

3. Jenny wants to buy a used car that her neighbor has for sale. However, she's $1,000 short of the $2,100 purchase price. Her bank is willing to lend her $1,000 at an annual interest rate of 15%, to be paid back over one year. Calculate the credit price of the car:

Cost of Buying the Car with Cash	Cash price of the car:	$_____
Cost of Buying the Car with Credit	Cash payment:	$_____
	Plus loan:	$_____
	Cost of credit:	$_____
	Cost of car with credit:	$_____

4. Visit a local bank and ask for a personal loan application. Fill out the application and bring it to class. Write a short essay analyzing whether you think the questions on the application fully capture a person's credit worthiness. Use a separate piece of paper if you need more space.

   _____

   _____

   _____

   _____

   _____

5. Use a mortgage calculator to solve the problems below. When you enter the interest rate of the mortgage loan and then the number of years it will take to pay it, the mortgage calculator will tell you how much your monthly mortgage payments would be.

Home Price	Down Payment	Mortgage	Years	Interest Rate	Monthly Mortgage Payment
$ 120,000	$ 12,000	$ 108,000	30	5%	$ _____
$ 300,000	$ 30,000	$ _____	30	4%	$ _____
$ 75,000	$ 7,500	$ _____	30	3%	$ _____

6. List the three steps involved in forecasting cash flow.

_____

_____

_____

_____

_____

_____

7. Name some methods involving credit and customer payments that businesses can use to improve cash flow.

_____

_____

_____

_____

_____

_____

8. List some inventory methods that businesses can use to improve cash flow.

_____

_____

_____

_____

Crossword

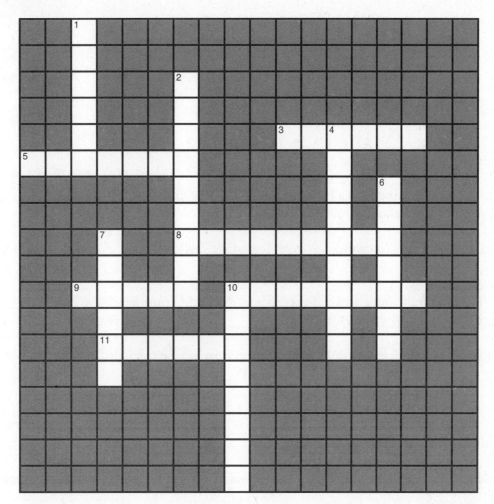

Use the clues below to solve the puzzle, which contains many vocabulary terms from Section 18.2.

Across

3. Money coming into a business is a cash _____

5. Money being spent in a business is a cash _____

8. One method to improve cash flow is to offer these to customers who pay in cash

9. Type of credit used when one business gives another business extended payment time for purchases

10. A person or business that grants time to pay off a debt

11. One of two steps involved in managing expenses

Down

1. A cash _____ is a record that forecasts cash flow for an upcoming period and compares actual cash flow to the forecasted amounts

2. One of two steps involved in managing expenses

4. Businesses typically collect this type of information from an applicant before granting credit

6. Credit _____ is a record of credit transactions

7. A credit _____ is a business that maintains credit records and sells the information under certain circumstances

10. Type of credit used when businesses offer the public extended payment time for purchases

Name _____ Class_____ Date _____

Check Yourself

In the sentences below, fill in the blanks with the correct answer.

1. One option for cutting expenses is to buy _____ equipment, instead of _____ equipment.

2. A sale made on credit is based on _____ that the person or business will pay the debt in the future.

3. Credit cards are issued by _____.

4. The cash that is coming into a business must be sufficient to cover the _____ that is flowing from the business.

5. All businesses should continuously work to reduce cash _____ and increase cash _____.

6. A new business that wants to keep expenses low should consider _____ buildings or company vehicles, rather than _____ them.

7. A cash budget includes columns for forecasted cash, actual cash, and the _____.

8. Business expenses are listed on the _____ statement.

Circle whether each statement is true or false.

9. True   False   Every person or business that has ever used credit has a credit history.

10. True   False   A person that buys something using credit is called a creditor.

11. True   False   Typical credit terms include a time limit and finance charges.

12. True   False   Merchants that accept credit cards pay no fees on these transactions.

13. True   False   Trade credit is credit granted by a business to another business.

14. True   False   Business owners use historical data to predict future cash flow.

15. True   False   New businesses often earn more cash than they spend at first.

16. True   False   A manager must be knowledgeable about the expenses the business incurs.

Extend Your Knowledge

The most difficult task in cash budgeting is accurately forecasting future cash inflows and outflows. Use the Internet to learn about variance analysis. Write a paper describing variance analysis and explaining how it can be used to improve forecasting accuracy in cash budgets. Make sure the paper is the length specified by the instructor.

STUDY GUIDE
Section 19.1

Managing Production & Distribution

Before You Begin

Think about the following question:

Would you like to run a business from your home?

Answer:　　☐ **Yes**　　　☐ **No**

If **Yes**, why would you like to run a business from your home?

_____

_____

_____

_____

_____

If **No**, why would you not like to run a business from your home?

_____

_____

_____

_____

_____

Who would be affected if you operated a business in your home?

_____

_____

_____

_____

_____

Concepts Review

1. What are the pros and cons of operating a business in one's home?

_____

_____

_____

_____

_____

_____

2. What factors should be considered when planning a layout?

_____

_____

_____

_____

_____

3. List the three issues on which production managers typically focus their attention.

_____

_____

4. What is the difference between a Gantt chart and a PERT chart?

_____

_____

_____

_____

5. Name some common measures of productivity for a small business.

_____

_____

6. What are some steps that production managers take to control quality?

_____

_____

_____

_____

7. Describe a typical distribution chain for a product.

_____

_____

_____

8. What is logistics?

_____

_____

_____

9. Explain the difference between a shipping department and a receiving department.

_____

_____

_____

10. Give some tips for handling goods when they are moved and stored.

_____

_____

_____

_____

_____

Name _____ Class_____ Date _____

Crossword

Use the clues below to solve the puzzle, which contains many vocabulary terms from Section 19.1.

Across

1. Price increase imposed by each seller in a distribution channel

3. What "FOB" stands for (3 words)

4. Chart that shows tasks as steps in a sequence and how they are dependent on each other

8. Local law that could forbid businesses in a residential area

9. Use of machines to perform tasks normally performed by people

10. Handling and organizing of materials, equipment, goods, and workers

11. Bar chart that shows the schedule of goals for a list of tasks

12. A distribution _____ is a series of steps through which products flow into or out of a business

Down

1. Significant point of progress in a process or timeline

2. Physical arrangement of objects and spaces

4. Measure of business output, such as the number of items created per employee

5. One of the issues that a production manager focuses on

6. A group of employees that suggests ways to improve the goods and services they produce (2 words)

7. The upkeep and routine care of equipment to keep it in working order

Name _____ Class_____ Date _____

Check Yourself

In the sentences below, fill in the blanks with the correct answer.

1. Businesses that use lots of machinery or have extensive product inventories will likely require a _____ space.

2. A schedule is not a wish list; it is a plan for achieving _____.

3. The goal of production management is to use materials and resources _____.

4. Productivity is a _____ of one numerical value to another numerical value.

5. Production managers monitor the performance of processes and _____.

6. The goal of distribution management is to ensure that products are _____, _____, and _____ in an organized, safe, and cost-effective way.

7. The price of a product in a retail store is typically much _____ than the original manufacturer's price.

8. An FOB location identifier indicates where ownership responsibility for a shipment switches from the _____ to the _____.

Circle whether each statement is true or false.

9. True   False   Some zoning laws forbid businesses in residential areas.

10. True   False   In small companies the business owner is often the production manager.

11. True   False   Production managers are responsible for ensuring that schedules are kept.

12. True   False   Gantt charts typically use circles to represent tasks.

13. True   False   An FOB location identifier is always the name of a city.

14. True   False   Automation is most common in the manufacturing industry.

15. True   False   The price of a product decreases as it goes along the distribution chain.

Extend Your Knowledge

Operations managers need to have good time management skills. Use the Internet to learn the steps commonly recommended for people who want to manage their time better. Write a paper describing these steps and how they could be used by a small business owner to improve his or her operations management. Make sure the paper is the length specified by the instructor.

STUDY GUIDE
Section 19.2

Managing Operations

Before You Begin

Think about the following question:

Has a sales clerk or cashier ever been rude to you?

Answer: ☐ **Yes**   ☐ **No**

If **Yes**, describe the incident.

_____

_____

_____

_____

_____

_____

If **Yes**, how did you feel about the business afterward?

_____

_____

_____

_____

_____

Why is it important for the employees of a business to be polite to customers?

_____

_____

_____

_____

Concepts Review

1. What is operations management?

_____

_____

_____

_____

2. Name some general policies that are common to most small businesses.

_____

_____

_____

_____

3. Why do retail businesses typically limit the hours they are open?

_____

_____

_____

_____

4. List and briefly describe each of the "Three C's."

_____

_____

_____

_____

5. What decisions should businesses make in determining their policies for dealing with returned goods?

_____

_____

_____

STUDY GUIDE 19.2

6. Why do businesses that sell products need delivery policies?

_____

_____

_____

_____

7. What is a customer service policy designed to do?

_____

_____

_____

_____

_____

8. Describe word of mouth and its effect on a business.

_____

_____

_____

_____

9. Name the five fundamental elements that govern the treatment of customers.

_____

_____

_____

_____

_____

10. What is credibility?

_____

_____

_____

_____

Crossword

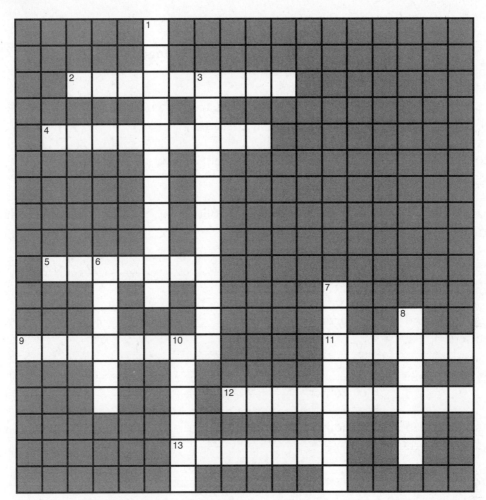

Use the clues below to solve the puzzle, which contains many vocabulary terms from Section 19.2.

Across

2. One of the "Three C's" that businesses rely on when deciding whether to extend credit to a customer

4. With 11 ACROSS, people who come back to a business again and again

5. One of the "Three C's" that businesses rely on when deciding whether to extend credit to a customer

9. Federal Express and UPS are examples of commercial _____ services

11. With 4 ACROSS, people who come back to a business again and again

12. Everyday activities that keep a business running

13. One of five fundamental elements governing the treatment of customers

Down

1. Verbal publicity that can be positive or negative (3 words)

3. The quality of being believable, trustworthy, and keeping one's promises

6. Procedure that specifies exactly how to accomplish something

7. Written statement from a seller that promises goods or services meet certain standards

8. Manufacturing term that refers to work performed to correct defects in a product

10. Businesses need to establish guidelines for allowing customers to _____ merchandise and receive a refund

Name _____ Class _____ Date _____

Check Yourself

In the sentences below, fill in the blanks with the correct answer.

1. Large businesses may devote an entire department to a single _____, such as sales, human resources, or production.

2. Businesses often rely on the "Three C's" when deciding whether to extend _____ to a particular customer.

3. A customer's past credit history is reviewed to help determine his or her _____.

4. Companies that sell products need to establish policies for handling situations when items are returned by _____ customers.

5. Rework policies state the conditions under which _____ products will be corrected.

6. Manufacturers and wholesalers commonly use _____ delivery services to ship large orders.

7. It costs more to gain a _____ customer than it does to keep an _____ customer.

8. A warranty describes the conditions under which particular _____ will be taken care of by the seller.

Circle whether each statement is true or false.

9. True   False   Small businesses may have only one person overseeing all operations.

10. True   False   Many business policies are in written form.

11. True   False   A business that is open 24/7 is open 24 hours a day for six days a week.

12. True   False   A delivery policy should include delivery options, costs, and a timetable.

13. True   False   A business without credibility builds customer loyalty.

14. True   False   A warranty is a legally binding document.

15. True   False   Dissatisfied customers are likely to be repeat customers.

Extend Your Knowledge

There are many stories on the Internet about businesses that provide poor customer service, but what about good customer service? Find a list of companies that are considered to have really good customer service. Give an oral presentation to the class describing what these companies do right and how this information can be useful to a small business owner. Make sure the presentation is the length specified by the instructor.

STUDY GUIDE
Section 20.1

Managing Purchasing

Before You Begin

Think about the following question:

What is your favorite store?

_____

Give at least two reasons why it is your favorite store.

_____

_____

_____

_____

_____

_____

Does your favorite store provide good value (that is good quality for the price)? Explain.

_____

_____

_____

_____

_____

_____

What would you do if your favorite store was out of whatever you wanted to buy?

_____

_____

_____

_____

_____

_____

Concepts Review

1. What kinds of things do businesses buy?

   _____

   _____

   _____

   _____

2. List the six goals of procurement management.

   _____

   _____

   _____

3. What are some of the components of quality to consider when purchasing a product?

   _____

   _____

   _____

   _____

4. Name some of the tools and sources that a purchasing manager uses to select the right quantity to buy.

   _____

   _____

   _____

5. Why is lead time an important concern in timing future purchases?

   _____

   _____

   _____

   _____

6. List the seven main factors involved in choosing a vendor.

_____

_____

_____

_____

7. Why is it difficult for small businesses to take advantage of very large quantity discounts?

_____

_____

_____

_____

_____

8. What is a reference date, and why is it important in trade credit?

_____

_____

_____

_____

_____

9. What is a cash discount?

_____

_____

_____

_____

10. List four types of paperwork common to the purchasing process.

_____

_____

_____

_____

Crossword

Use the clues below to solve the puzzle, which contains many vocabulary terms from Section 20.1.

Across

2. Choosing appropriate vendors to supply desired goods or services

5. Buyers who pay vendors in cash are often given a 1 to 3 percent _____

9. What the "M" stands for in "Net EOM"

10. Process for assessing the performance of a product relative to its cost (2 words)

11. E-procurement allows buyers to make purchases _____

12. Type of reordering used for items that are sold at a relatively constant rate

13. Type of discount given to resellers who are in the same industry as a vendor

Down

1. Period between order placement and receipt of shipment (2 words)

2. Product _____ is a written detailed description of a product

3. List of all items in a shipment (2 words)

4. Document issued by a vendor that lists items to be bought, quantities, prices, and other information (2 words)

6. Predicting future sales based on past data and expected market conditions is called sales _____

7. Type of discount given to buyers for purchasing a large amount of product

8. _____ procurement is purchasing goods and services that are environmentally beneficial

Check Yourself

In the sentences below, fill in the blanks with the correct answer.

1. Individuals who have purchasing responsibilities are called buyers, or purchasing _____.

2. When two items are equal in performance, the _____ item should be purchased.

3. The trade credit term "net 30" means payment is due within _____ days.

4. A vendor might give a quantity discount to a small business that commits to placing a _____ number of orders over a _____ time period.

5. The trade credit term "3/10 Net 60" means that full payment is due within _____ days, but a _____ discount is given if the bill is paid within the first _____ days of that period.

6. A _____ specification gives detailed information about an item that a buyer wants to buy.

7. Purchasing managers should make sure that _____, receipts, and packing slips are accurate and match the original purchase orders.

Circle whether each statement is true or false.

8. True   False   In small companies, the owner likely does all the purchasing.

9. True   False   A business that buys recycled-content paper practices green procurement.

10. True   False   Some businesses make purchasing decisions based on seasonal factors.

11. True   False   Buyers planning a purchase should get price quotes from several vendors.

12. True   False   Trade credit is the same as trade discount.

13. True   False   The trade credit abbreviation "EOM" stands for "every other month."

14. True   False   A cash discount typically ranges from 30% to 40% of the total due.

15. True   False   A purchase order is a document issued by a vendor to a buyer.

Extend Your Knowledge

You plan to start a business selling custom-designed silk-screened T-shirts. Use the Internet to locate at least five vendors from which you could purchase plain T-shirts. Conduct a value analysis to compare T-shirts from the different vendors. Write a paper describing your selection and value-analysis process. Make sure the paper is the length specified by the instructor.

Name _____ Class _____ Date _____

Managing Inventory

Before You Begin

Think about the following question:

Is there anything in your closet that you don't wear?

Answer: ☐ **Yes**   ☐ **No**

If **Yes**, why don't you ever wear it?

_____

_____

_____

_____

_____

_____

If **No**, what do you do with clothes you don't want anymore?

_____

_____

_____

_____

_____

_____

Name at least three ways you could free up space in your closet.

_____

_____

_____

_____

_____

_____

Concepts Review

1. What is the difference between inventory level, inventory value, and inventory investment?

   _____

   _____

   _____

2. Explain why the goal of inventory management is "not too little and not too much."

   _____

   _____

   _____

   _____

3. Name some of the data sources and considerations used in planning inventory level and investment.

   _____

   _____

   _____

4. How does a new business owner estimate how much inventory to have for opening day?

   _____

   _____

   _____

   _____

5. Explain how the terms "safety-stock level," "lead time," "reorder point," and "reorder level" are used in an inventory-level planning graph.

   _____

   _____

   _____

   _____

   _____

STUDY GUIDE 20.2

6. What is the formula for calculating average annual inventory investment?

_____

_____

_____

_____

7. Explain what it means to a business to have a low or high inventory turnover.

_____

_____

_____

_____

_____

8. What is the formula for calculating inventory turnover?

_____

_____

_____

_____

9. Name the causes of inventory shrinkage.

_____

_____

_____

_____

10. List five inventory systems.

_____

_____

_____

_____

Crossword

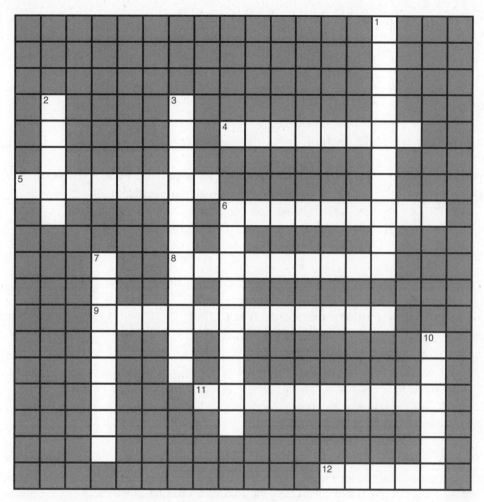

Use the clues below to solve the puzzle, which contains many vocabulary terms from Section 20.2.

Across

4. Inventory system that calculates inventory value at the end of the month or end of the year

5. Inventory _____ is the number of times in a given period that inventory is sold out and replaced

6. Stealing of small amounts of inventory over time

8. Inventory _____ is any loss that occurs between the time inventory is purchased and the time it is sold

9. Process of becoming no longer useful or desirable, such as inventory that is out of style

11. Where some businesses store and organize large quantities of inventory

12. Inventory _____ is the quantity of merchandise a business has available for sale

Down

1. What the "JIT" inventory system stands for (3 words)

2. Inventory _____ is the monetary worth of merchandise a business has available for sale

3. Minimum amount of inventory kept to meet high demand (2 words)

6. Inventory system that updates inventory value continually

7. This occurs when an item in inventory is completely gone (2 words)

10. Small businesses use this type of inventory system to count inventory items

STUDY GUIDE 20.2

Check Yourself

In the sentences below, fill in the blanks with the correct answer.

1. Inventory managers try to maintain inventory at a level that _____ customer demand, but _____ expenses.

2. Inventory management is closely linked with _____ management.

3. A high inventory turnover is good so long as it does not cause _____.

4. A business that wants an inventory turnover of 5 next year and plans to spend $1,000 on inventory next year should make an average inventory investment of _____.

5. One of the goals of inventory management is reconciling the _____ and _____ inventory levels.

6. Most businesses perform a physical inventory count at least _____ a year.

7. A partial inventory system combines elements of the _____ inventory system and the _____ inventory system.

8. The goal of the just-in-time inventory system is to keep almost _____ inventory in storage.

Circle whether each statement is true or false.

9. True   False   Inventory level affects how well a business can meet customer demand.

10. True   False   Inventory has a monetary value and a cost to a business.

11. True   False   A stock-out is good for business and pleases customers.

12. True   False   Obsolete inventory can be sold for much more than was paid for it.

13. True   False   The safety-stock level is the maximum amount of inventory allowed.

14. True   False   Pilfering and shoplifting decrease inventory levels.

15. True   False   The visual inventory system is commonly used by new small businesses.

16. True   False   A periodic inventory system calculates inventory value continually.

Extend Your Knowledge

Shoplifting and pilfering pose a major inventory shrinkage problem. Use Internet resources to learn tips about preventing shoplifting and pilfering. Focus on prevention methods useful to small business owners. Present your findings to the class in a PowerPoint presentation. Make sure the presentation is the length specified by the instructor.

STUDY GUIDE
Section 21.1

Planning for Business Growth

Before You Begin

Think about the following question:

Do you have hobbies?

Answer:　☐ **Yes**　　☐ **No**

If **Yes**, what are your hobbies and how much time and money do you put into them?

_____

_____

_____

_____

_____

_____

If **No**, why don't you have hobbies?

_____

_____

_____

_____

_____

Assume hobbies are a form of personal growth engaged in by people who have the time and money to devote to them. Relate this concept to business growth.

_____

_____

_____

_____

_____

_____

Concepts Review

1. Explain the difference between internal and external business growth.

_____

_____

_____

_____

_____

2. Name the three factors that affect the decision to grow a business.

_____

_____

_____

3. Do you agree with the concept that a quality product will make a business successful in the long run? Explain your thinking.

_____

_____

_____

_____

_____

4. Do you believe in paying more for higher-quality products or in buying cheaper ones? Give an example of a high-quality product, and explain how you would recognize it.

_____

_____

_____

_____

_____

5. Why is it important for a business to understand a product group's stage in the product life cycle before offering a new product for sale from that group?

_____

_____

_____

_____

6. List the three broad categories of growth strategies.

_____

_____

_____

7. Name the three most common types of intensive growth strategies.

_____

_____

_____

8. What are the two goals of market penetration?

_____

_____

_____

9. Describe the difference between market development and product development.

_____

_____

_____

_____

_____

10. List the two types of integrative growth strategies.

_____

_____

Crossword

Use the clues below to solve the puzzle, which contains many vocabulary terms from Section 21.1.

Across

1. Type of 9 ACROSS in which a business adds new products that are *not* related to its existing products

6. Type of 9 ACROSS in which a business adds new products that *are* related to its existing products

7. The most important focus of a company is its _____ business

9. Growth strategy in which a business grows by offering products that are different from its established product line

12. A series of stages a product may pass through while it's on the market (2 words)

13. Growth strategy for creating new products or enhancing existing ones is product _____

Down

2. Type of growth strategy that blends businesses through acquisitions and mergers

3. _____ growth is expanding a business internally by adding products or services

4. The first stage a product passes through when it comes on the market

5. Type of 12 ACROSS in which a product remains in the maturity stage forever

8. Market _____ is a growth strategy that markets a product intensively

10. Percentage of the total sales captured by a product is the market _____

11. The final stage a product passes through while it's on the market

Name _____ Class _____ Date _____

Check Yourself

In the sentences below, fill in the blanks with the correct answer.

1. Before growing a business the business owner should update the original _____ or develop an entirely new one.

2. Growing a business is not only an economic move, but a _____ one as well.

3. During the _____ stage of a product life cycle the sales and profits will level off and may start to decline.

4. Items in common everyday use over a long time period are said to have a _____ life cycle.

5. "Doing more of what you are good at doing" describes the _____ growth strategy.

6. One goal of market penetration is to convince existing customers to buy your product _____ often.

7. Intensive growth strategies are typically _____ expensive than integrative growth strategies.

Circle whether each statement is true or false.

8. True   False   Most small businesses that expand do it through internal growth.

9. True   False   A business is likely ready to expand when it makes a consistent profit.

10. True   False   An economic downturn is always a bad time to expand a business.

11. True   False   The introduction stage of a product life cycle is typically expensive.

12. True   False   All product life-cycle curves have the same shape.

13. True   False   Market share is usually expressed as a percentage.

14. True   False   A wholesaler that buys another wholesaler is practicing vertical integration.

15. True   False   The core business of a gasoline station is selling food.

Extend Your Knowledge

Although entrepreneurs may find it easy to set their goals for business and professional growth, setting life goals can be much more difficult. Use the Internet to learn about life goals and how to set them. Give an oral presentation to the class describing what you have learned. Make sure the presentation is the length specified by the instructor.

STUDY GUIDE 21.2

STUDY GUIDE
Section 21.2

Challenges of Growth

Before You Begin

Think about the following question:

Do you believe the saying, "If you want something done right, do it yourself"?

Answer: ☐ **Yes**   ☐ **No**

If **Yes**, why do you believe the saying is true?

_____

_____

_____

_____

If **No**, why do you believe the saying is not true?

_____

_____

_____

_____

Would it be difficult for a business owner that believes this saying to expand his or her small business? Explain.

_____

_____

_____

_____

_____

_____

Name _____ Class _____ Date _____

Concepts Review

1. Describe the entrepreneurial mindset.

_____

_____

_____

2. Name some of the disadvantages of growing a business.

_____

_____

_____

_____

3. Name some of the advantages of growing a business.

_____

_____

_____

_____

4. Describe a micromanager.

_____

_____

_____

_____

5. List six practical challenges of growing a business.

_____

_____

_____

_____

6. Why does a growing business usually need more IT?

_____

_____

_____

_____

_____

7. Name the three options for financing business growth.

_____

_____

_____

_____

8. List the four categories considered in a SWOT analysis.

_____

_____

_____

9. What are the primary factors to consider as part of the threat component of a SWOT analysis for a business-growth opportunity?

_____

_____

_____

_____

_____

10. What are potential drawbacks of opening a new, second location of a successful business?

_____

_____

_____

_____

_____

Crossword

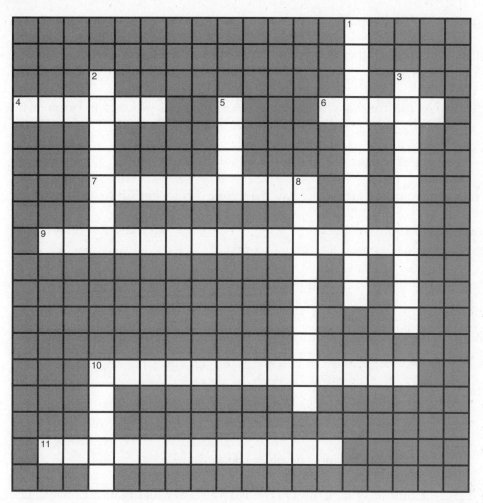

Use the clues below to solve the puzzle, which contains many vocabulary terms from Section 21.2.

Across

4. Money obtained from an investor in exchange for business ownership is _____ capital

6. One of the practical challenges of growing a business

7. Growing a business might involve needing to change the organizational _____

9. With 2 DOWN, an optimistic, can-do attitude needed to create a business

10. Obtaining funds for growth from existing operations (2 words)

11. Business owner who interferes in the decisions and tasks of employees

Down

1. With 3 DOWN, what "IT" stands for

2. With 9 ACROSS, an optimistic, can-do attitude needed to create a business

3. With 1 DOWN, what "IT" stands for

5. Money obtained by a business through a loan is _____ capital

8. What a growing business might need to purchase

10. One of the practical challenges of growing a business

STUDY GUIDE 21.2

Check Yourself

In the sentences below, fill in the blanks with the correct answer.

1. The entrepreneurial mindset is ideal for starting a new business, but may not be as useful when it comes to _____ the business.

2. Business owners must ultimately make the decision about whether to grow or not based on their _____ goals.

3. A growing business usually requires more physical _____.

4. A business that wants to grow may have to train existing staff in new _____.

5. Debt capital and equity capital are _____ sources of money for growth, while self-financing is an _____ source.

6. Knowing your business's capabilities, limitations, and threats will help you select an appropriate _____ opportunity.

7. A business owner considering growing his or her business should prepare a new _____ plan to assess all aspects of the situation.

Circle whether each statement is true or false.

8. True   False   A micromanager trusts his or her employees to get jobs done right.

9. True   False   Growing a business involves taking on risk.

10. True   False   A business that grows may have to change its organizational structure.

11. True   False   A growing business usually requires less employees.

12. True   False   A SWOT analysis should be used to analyze growth opportunities.

13. True   False   The entrepreneurial mindset includes a negative pessimistic outlook.

14. True   False   Business growth requires financing.

Extend Your Knowledge

Growing a business is nearly impossible for a business owner who is a micromanager and refuses to delegate some of his or her responsibilities to employees within the firm or to outside specialists. Use Internet resources to learn about delegating. Which tasks should small business owners typically delegate to others? How should managers carry out the delegating process? How does delegating benefit the business owner and the employees of the business? Report your findings in a paper. Make sure the paper is the length specified by the instructor.

STUDY GUIDE
Section 22.1

Franchising & Licensing

Before You Begin

Think about the following question:

Are fast food restaurants dependable?

Answer: ☐ Yes   ☐ No

Define dependable.

_____

_____

_____

_____

_____

Why do you expect the look, packaging, and foods in a fast food restaurant to be very similar at all the locations of that restaurant with the same name?

_____

_____

_____

_____

_____

How do you feel about the dependability of non-franchised, locally owned restaurants?

_____

_____

_____

_____

_____

Concepts Review

1. List three payments typically paid by a franchisee to a franchisor.

_____

_____

2. Summarize the information that must be included in a franchise disclosure document.

_____

_____

_____

3. Summarize the information that must be included in a franchise agreement.

_____

_____

_____

_____

4. Summarize the information that must be included in a franchise operations manual.

_____

_____

_____

5. For each franchise in the table, use the formula (Royalties = Royalty Fee × Sales) to calculate how much you would owe the franchisor in royalties if you made one million dollars in sales:

Franchise	Franchise Fee	Start-Up Costs	Royalty Fee	Royalties Owed
McDonald's	$ 45,000	$ 489,000–$ 1.5 million	12.5%	$ _____
Arby's LLC	$ 25,000–$ 37,500	$ 333,000–$ 2 million	4%	$ _____
GNC Franchising Inc.	$ 30,000	$ 132,000–$ 182,000	6%	$ _____
Tastee-Freez LLC	$ 5,000	$ 39,000	4%	$ _____

6. List the five major advantages to a franchisor of franchising his or her business.

_____

_____

_____

7. List the five major disadvantages to a franchisor of franchising his or her business.

_____

_____

_____

8. What are the responsibilities of a brand licensee?

_____

_____

_____

_____

9. List the nine typical components of a licensing agreement.

_____

_____

_____

_____

_____

_____

10. List the two major advantages to a brand licensor of licensing a brand.

_____

_____

11. List five potential problems for a brand licensor to licensing a brand.

_____

_____

_____

Crossword

Use the clues below to solve the puzzle, which contains many vocabulary terms from Section 22.1.

Across

2. Choosing the wrong product to brand

4. Type of legal document that provides information to a franchisee about the franchisor

6. What the "F" in "FTC" stands for

8. Legally and financially responsible

10. A franchise _____ gives detailed instructions on how to run a franchise unit (2 words)

11. Type of fund franchisees pay into for radio and TV promotion

12. Perceived monetary value of a brand

Down

1. What the "T" in "FTC" stands for

3. Protection in an agreement from legal action, fines, or damages

5. Percentage of sales earned that is paid to a franchisor

7. Market _____ occurs when a product has been completely distributed in its market

8. Granting permission to a person or company to use a brand

9. A franchise _____ is a legally binding contract between franchisor and franchisee

Check Yourself

In the sentences below, fill in the blanks with the correct answer.

1. A franchisee uses another company's name and operation to run the same business in another _____.

2. A franchise disclosure document must typically be given to a potential franchisee at least _____ days before the franchisee signs a franchise agreement or pays the franchise fee.

3. A franchise agreement describes the _____ territory in which a franchisee can operate.

4. A business can expand geographically by opening multiple company-owned units or by _____ the business.

5. Franchising builds _____ awareness for the franchisor's products or services.

6. A licensee may have to provide regular samples of branded products so the licensor can make sure they meet _____-control standards.

Circle whether each statement is true or false.

7. True   False   A franchisor is the owner of an established company.

8. True   False   A franchise fee is typically only a few hundred dollars.

9. True   False   A franchise agreement typically has a term limit, for example, 10 years.

10. True   False   A franchise operations manual must be detailed and precise.

11. True   False   A franchisor is liable for accidents in a franchise location.

12. True   False   A business owner with a struggling business should franchise it.

13. True   False   A potential brand licensee wants a brand with a poor reputation.

14. True   False   A brand licensor maintains ownership of the brand name.

Extend Your Knowledge

Franchising and licensing agreements are complex legal contracts. Disputes between a franchisor and franchisee or between a brand licensor and brand licensee arise when one party feels that the other party has not lived up to the conditions of the contract. Such disputes are commonly handled through one of three methods—mediation, arbitration, or litigation. Write a paper in which you describe and compare these three methods. How are they used to settle the kinds of disputes that arise in franchising and licensing? What are the advantages and disadvantages of each method for settling such disputes? Make sure the paper is the length specified by the instructor.

STUDY GUIDE 22.1

STUDY GUIDE
Section 22.2

Exit Strategies

Before You Begin

Think about the following question:

Will you ever stop working?

Answer: ☐ **Yes**   ☐ **No**

If **Yes**, at what age do you think you will stop working?

_____

_____

_____

_____

If **No**, why do you think you will work the rest of your life?

_____

_____

_____

_____

_____

_____

How can you be sure you will have the financial resources to stop working some day?

_____

_____

_____

_____

_____

Concepts Review

1. List the three factors that a business owner should consider when deciding to sell a business.

   _____

2. Name the factors that a business owner should consider when valuing his or her business.

   _____

   _____

3. Describe the liquidation process and when it is used.

   _____

   _____

4. Give the formulas for two business-valuation methods.

   _____

   _____

5. List some intangible positive aspects that a business may have.

   _____

   _____

6. Explain the difference between an acquisition and a merger.

   _____

   _____

7. List some harvesting options for the owners of privately held companies.

   _____

8. Explain the relationship between reward, risk, and rate of growth for investments.

   _____

9. Explain the Future Value of Money chart.

   _____

   _____

10. What four questions should you never stop asking yourself?

_____

_____

_____

11. Gina earns $50 per week babysitting. How much will she have left to spend each week after saving ten percent? How much will she save in a month?.

_____

12. You deposit $1,000 in your bank at a 6% interest rate. How much will you have in a year?

_____

13. How long will it take for $120 to double if the annual return on investment is 12%?

_____

14. Give two factors that affect the risk associated with an investment.

_____

15. Use the Future Value of Money chart on p. 595 in the textbook to calculate the following:

    a. $100 for 5 periods at 5% _____

    b. $1 for 10 periods at 12% _____

    c. $1,000 for 11 periods at 6% _____

16. A rule of thumb is that a business can be sold for about three times its net annual profit. Using that rule, fill in the chart below for the following businesses:

Business	Average Yearly Profit	Estimate Sale Price
Website design	$ 4,000	$ _____
Aquarium cleaning	$ 1,000	$ _____
DJ service	$ 7,500	$ _____
Clothing boutique	$ 30,000	$ _____

Crossword

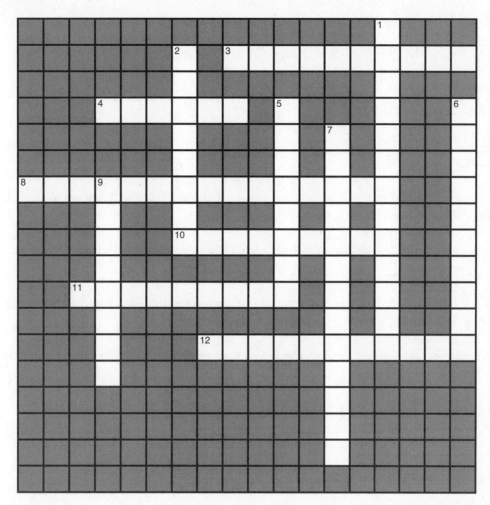

Use the clues below to solve the puzzle, which contains many vocabulary terms from Section 22.2.

Across

3. What the "R" in "IRA" stands for

4. In a management _____, a business owner sells his ownership shares to his managers

8. Method of decreasing risk by spreading your money over several types of investments

10. The ease of converting a non-cash asset into cash

11. A business's worth based on total assets minus total liabilities (2 words)

12. How invested money grows when you earn interest on your interest

Down

1. Cash saved to cover personal expenses for several months (2 words)

2. Business term for valuation that refers to the intangible positive aspects of a business

5. Stocks or other investments that are changeable and unpredictable are described as _____

6. Exiting a business and gaining its value in cash

7. An IPO is a(n) _____ offering (2 words)

9. What the "E" in "ESOP" stands for

Check Yourself

In the sentences below, fill in the blanks with the correct answer.

1. Growing money by earning interest on your interest is called _____.

2. Spreading your money over different types of investments to reduce risk is _____.

3. You should get into the habit of automatically saving _____ percent of your income.

4. The rule of 72 states that _____ divided by the interest or rate of return equals the number of years needed to _____ an investment.

5. Your emergency fund should contain enough cash to cover your personal expenses for at least _____ months.

6. Stocks are considered _____ investments, because their prices change frequently and unpredictably.

7. Once you have saved some money and know your risk tolerance, you are almost ready to _____.

Circle whether each statement is true or false.

8. True   False   One of the goals of owning a business is to build personal wealth.

9. True   False   There is a simple formula for calculating the value of a business.

10. True   False   The value of goodwill associated with a business cannot be calculated.

11. True   False   Cash investments are much riskier than stocks and bonds.

12. True   False   You should invest money so it can earn more money.

13. True   False   Risky investments usually grow slowly and offer low rewards.

14. True   False   Diversification means "putting all your eggs in one basket."

15. True   False   You have the power to think for yourself.

Extend Your Knowledge

One of the most exciting possibilities about being an entrepreneur is building wealth. What would you do with that wealth? How would it benefit you, your family, your community, or the world? Share your vision with the class through an oral presentation. Include specific examples of how you would use your wealth, who would benefit from it, and how they would benefit. Make sure the presentation is the length specified by the instructor.

Business Plan Project

BUSINESS PLAN PROJECT
Section 1.1

What Is Entrepreneurship?

Before you begin this course—and begin developing a business plan for your own business—let's see how much you already know about entrepreneurship.

For each question, circle the answer that best represents how you think. In some cases, several may seem very close, but choose just one.

1. An entrepreneur is someone

   A. Who has an idea for a business.

   B. Who starts a business.

   C. Who works for him- or herself and has no employees.

   D. Who has started a company and has 3 employees.

2. Entrepreneurs are people who

   A. Want to take control of a situation.

   B. Are not willing to take advice from other people.

   C. Are only thinking of their own welfare.

   D. Are willing to work all hours to please a client.

3. All entrepreneurs want to grow their businesses.

   A. True

   B. False

4. Companies started by entrepreneurs typically have

   A. Fewer than 10 employees.

   B. 11 to 100 employees.

   C. 100 or more employees.

   D. Varying numbers of employees.

5. Getting a steady paycheck and working a set number of hours a week is a benefit of being

   A. An employee.

   B. An entrepreneur.

   C. Either an employee or an entrepreneur.

   D. Neither an employee nor an entrepreneur.

6. Entrepreneurs start one company and stay with it their entire working career.

    A. True

    B. False

7. Generally, entrepreneurs are willing to take risks

    A. In almost every situation, no matter what the cost.

    B. In situations where the reward outweighs the risk.

    C. Rarely or only when the business is faced with disaster.

    D. Never.

8. Entrepreneurs can start businesses in almost any type of industry and provide services, products, or both.

    A. True

    B. False

9. There are a number of rewards associated with being an entrepreneur. Which of the following is most important?

    A. Financial security.

    B. Not having to make the rules or take responsibility.

    C. Doing something you love.

    D. Working as much or as little as you want to in order to make a living.

10. For entrepreneurs to be successful, they should

    A. Pay attention to new technology and take advantage of it, if possible.

    B. Be aware of what's going on in the world in terms of social, business, political, and environmental trends

    C. Pick a business that they enjoy.

    D. Have strict rules on what can and cannot be done.

BUSINESS PLAN PROJECT 1.1

Evaluation

For each of the questions, circle the number that corresponds to the letter you chose as your answer. For example, on Question 1 if you had circled "A" as your answer, then you would circle "0" opposite Question 1 and below "A."

When you have finished, add up your total and write it on the last line of the grid.

Section 1.1	Your Answer A	Your Answer B	Your Answer C	Your Answer D
Question 1	0	2	2	2
Question 2	3	0	0	3
Question 3	0	1		
Question 4	1	1	1	3
Question 5	3	0	0	0
Question 6	1	0		
Question 7	1	3	1	0
Question 8	1	0		
Question 9	0	0	2	2
Question 10	2	2	2	0
Totals				
Total for Assessment 1.1 _____				

If Your Total Was 16 or More

You have an excellent understanding of entrepreneurship. You understand the types of companies entrepreneurs start, as well as the risks and rewards of entrepreneurship. You recognize the differences between being an entrepreneur and an employee, and understand some of the factors that can help make entrepreneurs successful.

If Your Total Was 8 to 15

You have a good understanding of what entrepreneurship involves. Entrepreneurship is a world where people can start their own businesses and pick what they'd like to do. It's also a world that has a number of challenges. To most people who become entrepreneurs, the rewards outweigh the challenges.

If Your Total Was 7 or Less

Being an entrepreneur has both its challenges and rewards. As you learn more about entrepreneurship in this course, you'll have a better understanding of both. It's only when you really understand what entrepreneurship involves that you'll be able to make a decision about whether it's something you want to pursue. Meanwhile, take this opportunity to learn all you can. The concepts that are involved can help you in any business endeavor you undertake.

BUSINESS PLAN PROJECT 1.1

BUSINESS PLAN PROJECT
Section 1.2

Characteristics of an Entrepreneur

Do you know whether you have the characteristics and skills necessary to be an entrepreneur? As you answer the following questions, you'll begin to realize whether being an entrepreneur is for you.

For each question, circle the answer that best represents how you think. In some cases, several may seem very close, but choose just one.

1. You're working on a project for a client and the due day is tomorrow. In order to finish it on time, you need to work most of the night, but you've made a date to see a friend. What would you do?

   A. Cancel your date with your friend and work all night to finish the project.

   B. Call your client and tell him you have a family emergency and will get the finished project to him as soon as you can.

   C. Meet your friend for a short time and enlist his/her help in finishing the project.

   D. Postpone your date and do as much work as you're able to, recognizing that you may have to apologize to your client the next day because the project isn't finished.

2. Having a positive attitude is important to being a successful entrepreneur.

   A. True

   B. False

3. What's most important to being successful as an entrepreneur?

   A. Having a dream.

   B. Being able to motivate yourself.

   C. Having certain skills.

   D. Being able to follow directions.

4. The business you started a year ago has hit a roadblock and you don't think you can overcome it. The economy has tanked and people are just not interested in spending any money on your service. You realize that the best thing to do is to close your business. How do you think you would feel about going out of business?

   A. It's a terrible tragedy and it will bother you for some time.

   B. It reflects something that you did wrong and you don't want anyone to know about it.

   C. Businesses close all the time. It's unfortunate but nothing earth-shattering.

   D. It was a learning experience and you can use the information in your next business.

5. When you're trying to solve problems, are you more comfortable solving them

   A. On your own.

   B. Working with a team.

   C. Leading the team to solve the problem.

   D. Depending on other people to solve the problem and then using the solution.

6. Entrepreneurs are born with all the qualities they need to be successful.

   A. True

   B. False

7. You've always had part-time jobs from babysitting to walking dogs or washing cars. The money you've made has helped you buy things that you want and given you a sense of financial security. If you suddenly had no clients for these jobs, how would you feel?

   A. A bit upset but you think you could find other clients.

   B. A bit upset but you think you could get other types of jobs and replace the income.

   C. A bit upset but you decide you can cut down on some of your expenses and that you could do without that income.

   D. Very upset. You couldn't stand not having the security of having that income.

8. You have been working for the XYZ Corporation for two years doing video editing. The company is about to downsize its video department and is offering everyone who works in the department two options. One option is to stay without benefits; the other option is to leave and get severance (payment for leaving). You've been thinking about starting your own business doing video editing but you're not quite sure you're ready to go out on your own. Which of the following options would you pick?

   A. Stay with XYZ without benefits. You want another year of experience before you go out on your own.

   B. Leave and get severance and ask XYZ for a contract to do a certain amount of video editing over the next year.

   C. This is the opportunity you've been waiting for. Take the severance and start your own business.

9. You're daydreaming about your future life in business. You see yourself

   A. Earning tons of money and buying everything you want.

   B. Working all hours of the day and night, utterly fulfilled by your work.

   C. Doing something you love and making a living as well.

   D. Having a secure job that you like that provides a good living.

BUSINESS PLAN PROJECT 1.2

10. You have to get hold of someone for an interview. He hasn't responded to the first message you left on his phone. Would you

   A. Call one more time and leave another message. If he doesn't respond, you figure he's just not that interested in the interview.

   B. Call several more times hoping that he'll pick up the phone.

   C. Call several more times and leave one more message. Meanwhile try to find out his email and contact him that way.

   D. Not bother calling any more. He has your number and he can call you.

Evaluation

For each of the questions, circle the number that corresponds to the letter you chose as your answer. For example, on Question 1 if you had circled "A" as your answer, then you would circle "2" opposite Question 1 and below "A."

When you have finished, add up your total and write it on the last line of the grid.

Section 1.2	Your Answer A	Your Answer B	Your Answer C	Your Answer D
Question 1	2	0	1	2
Question 2	1	0		
Question 3	2	2	1	0
Question 4	1	0	2	3
Question 5	3	1	2	0
Question 6	0	1		
Question 7	2	2	1	0
Question 8	0	2	1	
Question 9	1	2	2	0
Question 10	1	2	3	0
Totals				
Total for Assessment 1.2 _____				

If Your Total Was 16 or More

Congratulations! You're ready to become an entrepreneur. You have many of the personal characteristics needed to be successful—from determination to discipline. And your enthusiasm about business indicates a motivation for achievement.

If Your Total Was 8 to15

You're on your way to becoming an entrepreneur! You have some of the personal characteristics needed to be successful. You can develop others with just a little bit of work. Learning more about business, finance, and career paths will increase your potential.

If Your Total Was 7 or Less

Even though you may not have all the characteristics necessary to be an entrepreneur right now, you can develop many of them. Becoming an entrepreneur is not necessarily the right choice for everyone. Many of the things you'll learn in this course can help you whether you work for someone else or for yourself. Having a positive attitude and believing in yourself are the most important traits for success.

Working on Your Business Plan

What skills do I have to start this business?

Business Idea

1. Describe your business idea.

_____

_____

_____

_____

_____

If you haven't yet settled on a business opportunity, here's a way to come up with one. It requires a partner.

a. List any ideas for businesses that you could imagine starting.

_____

_____

_____

b. Ask your partner about his or her interests, skills, hobbies, and work experience. Then write a list of the businesses you could imagine your partner starting, based on what you've learned. Ask your partner to do the same for you.

_____

_____

_____

c. Compare your list of businesses you could imagine starting with your partner's list of businesses he or she could imagine you starting. Are there any businesses on both lists? Do you like some of your partner's ideas better than your own? Or, would you choose an idea from your own list? Either way, you need to choose one business opportunity for this project. Describe that business:

_____

_____

_____

Business Name

2. What will you name your business?

_____

_____

_____

Academic and Work Qualifications

3. Describe any academic and work qualifications that relate to your new business.

_____

_____

_____

_____

_____

_____

_____

_____

Personal Characteristics and Skills

4. Describe any personal characteristics and skills that relate to your new business.

_____

_____

_____

_____

_____

_____

_____

_____

_____

Entrepreneurial Characteristics

5. From the list of characteristics below, check the three that you think are your strongest. These will be used when you begin developing the first section of your business plan.

Characteristic	Explanation	One of My Three Strongest?
Drive	Highly motivated	
Perseverance	Sticking to task or goal	
Risk-Taking	Willing to take chances	
Organization	Life and work in order	
Confidence	Sure of yourself	
Persuasiveness	Able to convince others	
Honesty	Open, truthful	
Competitiveness	Eager to win	
Adaptability	Coping with new situations	
Understanding	Empathy with others	
Discipline	Self-control	
Vision	Able to keep goals in mind	

BUSINESS PLAN PROJECT
Section 2.1

Importance of Entrepreneurship in the Economy

When it comes to economics—the flow of goods and services between people—everyone has questions. How much should something cost? Why are some items so expensive? Why is the price going down? As you answer the following questions, you'll have an idea of how economics affects everyone—from entrepreneurs to consumers.

For each question, circle the answer that best represents how you think. In some cases, several may seem very close, but choose just one.

1. When a store puts an item on sale, it is lowering the cost because

    A. It can't sell the item at its usual retail cost.

    B. It wants to bring more shoppers into the store.

    C. New items are coming in.

    D. All of the above

2. In the United States, who ultimately decides what the price of most products will be?

    A. The manufacturer who makes the product.

    B. The retailer who sells the product.

    C. The consumers who buy the product.

    D. The government.

3. The price of a dress may go up when

    A. It represents the latest style.

    B. There are only a few dresses available.

    C. The manufacturer needs to make more money.

    D. All of the above

4. The price for Mother's Day cards would be highest

    A. The day after Mother's Day.

    B. The day before Mother's Day.

    C. Two weeks before Mother's Day.

    D. Two weeks after Mother's Day.

BUSINESS PLAN PROJECT 2.1

5. Many people think that price reflects quality, and that the more you pay for something, the more it is worth. Do you think this is true

   A. All of the time

   B. Most of the time

   C. Some of the time

   D. Never

6. If companies don't make a profit, they can't stay in business

   A. True

   B. False

7. When is fresh lettuce most expensive?

   A. In the summer

   B. In the fall

   C. In the winter

8. When is a book most expensive?

   A. Just after it's been published.

   B. When it comes out in paperback.

   C. When it is out-of-print and only a few copies are available.

   D. When it is remaindered.

9. Non-profits are businesses

   A. That want to make money.

   B. That are more interested in performing a service to benefit people than making money.

   C. That both want to make money and perform a service.

10. When several companies make the same product or offer the same service, they're competing against each other. Competition among suppliers helps the

    A. Prices of goods and services to go down.

    B. Prices of goods and services to go up.

    C. Prices of goods and services to stay the same.

Evaluation

For each of the questions, circle the number that corresponds to the letter you chose as your answer. For example, on Question 1 if you had circled "A" as your answer, then you would circle "1" opposite Question 1 and below "A."

When you have finished, add up your total and write it on the last line of the grid.

Section 2.1	Your Answer A	Your Answer B	Your Answer C	Your Answer D
Question 1	1	1	1	3
Question 2	0	0	3	0
Question 3	1	1	1	3
Question 4	0	2	1	0
Question 5	0	1	2	0
Question 6	1	0	--	--
Question 7	0	1	2	--
Question 8	2	1	3	0
Question 9	0	3	0	--
Question 10	3	0	0	--
Totals				
Total for Assessment 2.1 _____				

If Your Total Was 16 or More

You have an excellent understanding of the basics of economics and how prices reflect supply and demand. You also have a good grasp of profit and competition. You can look forward to using your knowledge in whatever business venture you undertake.

If Your Total Was 8 to 15

You have a good understanding of the basics of economics, which will serve you well in your future endeavors. Learning more about economics is always a good idea since it is a major factor in both your business and personal finances.

If Your Total Was 7 or Less

Understanding various concepts in economics can be difficult the first time through. As you go through the following chapter, many of these concepts will become clear and, with a little work, you'll find that you have a good grasp of them.

Name _____ Class _____ Date _____

 Working on Your Business Plan

What factors will influence the demand for my product or service?

1. Think about the business that you would like to start. What factors will influence the *demand* for your product or service?

_____

_____

_____

_____

_____

_____

_____

_____

_____

_____

2. What factors will influence the *supply* for your product or service?

_____

_____

_____

_____

_____

_____

_____

_____

_____

BUSINESS PLAN PROJECT
Section 2.2

Thinking Globally, Acting Locally

The global economy—the flow of goods and services around the world—affects the prices we pay for almost everything. The following questions will give you an idea of how much you already know about the global economy.

For each question, circle the answer that best represents how you think. In some cases, several may seem very close, but choose just one.

1. U.S. imports are goods that are

    A. Manufactured abroad and brought into the United States.

    B. Manufactured in the United States and sold around the world.

    C. Manufactured in the United States and sold in the United States.

    D. Manufactured abroad and not sold in the United States.

2. A local economy is a

    A. Limited geographical area.

    B. State or group of states.

    C. Country.

    D. Place where everyone uses the same currency.

3. The global economy is possible because of

    A. The Internet.

    B. Multiple means of transporting goods around the world.

    C. The needs of some nations to get goods and services they can't produce.

    D. All of the above

4. Most nations specialize in making goods and providing services.

    A. True

    B. False

5. Exported goods from the United States are least expensive in other countries when

    A. The dollar is strong.

    B. The dollar is weak.

    C. No trade barriers exist.

BUSINESS PLAN PROJECT 2.2

6. Easy and quick transportation of goods from one place to another makes the global economy possible. If you were going to bring cutting-edge fashions from China to the United States, would you choose

   A. The fastest but most expensive way of transportation, which would enable the fashions to be sold at the beginning of the season?

   B. A slower and less expensive way of transportation that would bring them in at the middle of the buying season?

   C. The slowest and least expensive means of shipping which would bring the fashions in after the season?

7. A quota limits the quantity of a product that can be imported into a country. Quotas in the United States are imposed because

   A. American manufacturers of the same goods don't want the competition.

   B. Foreign made goods are never of the same quality as U.S. goods.

   C. The wages paid to the workers in the foreign factory are much, much lower than U.S. wages.

8. Harry James has a small company that designs T-shirts. He wants to get his T-shirts manufactured as inexpensively as possible but at as high a quality as possible. To find the best possible suppliers, he should

   A. Check the Internet.

   B. Go to Trade Fairs that attract manufacturers from around the world.

   C. Ask for samples from potential suppliers.

   D. All of the above

9. The exchange rate between the currencies of different countries varies constantly.

   A. True

   B. False

10. Hector wants his business to not harm the environment. Therefore, he makes sure he only uses

   A. Recyclable packaging.

   B. Organic products.

   C. Eco-friendly raw materials.

   D. All the above

Evaluation

For each of the questions, circle the number that corresponds to the letter you chose as your answer. For example, on Question 1 if you had circled "A" as your answer, then you would circle "3" opposite Question 1 and below "A."

When you have finished, add up your total and write it on the last line of the grid.

Section 2.2	Your Answer A	Your Answer B	Your Answer C	Your Answer D
Question 1	3	0	0	0
Question 2	3	0	0	0
Question 3	1	2	3	3
Question 4	1	0	--	--
Question 5	0	2	1	--
Question 6	2	1	0	--
Question 7	2	0	0	--
Question 8	1	1	1	3
Question 9	1	0	--	--
Question 10	1	1	1	3
Totals				
Total for Assessment 2.2 _____				

If Your Total Was 16 or More

You have an excellent understanding of the basics of the global economy and the concepts of international trade. You should be able to apply these concepts when discussing various businesses and the reasons why they succeed or fail.

If Your Total Was 8 to 15

You have a good understanding of the global economy. This knowledge is becoming more and more important as many entrepreneurs operate in a world-wide marketplace.

If Your Total Was 7 or Less

Understanding the global economy is a new field of study for many people and many of the concepts can be unfamiliar. As you start learning about the global economy, you'll recognize how it affects you on a day-to-day basis.

BUSINESS PLAN PROJECT 2.2

BUSINESS PLAN PROJECT
Section 3.1

Types of Business

You've learned about the four broad categories of business. The following questions will give you an idea of how you feel about each one.

For each question, circle the answer that best represents how you think. In some cases, several may seem very close, but choose just one.

1. Being able to put things together is essential in manufacturing.

   A. All manufacturers make a product from beginning to end.

   B. Many manufacturers make one part of a product.

   C. Many manufacturers assemble a product from parts made by other companies.

   D. Both B and C

2. Dealing with customers is important in the retail industries. What would you do if a customer walked into your shop and was angry about an article of clothing she bought, saying that it didn't look good on her. You have a "no refund" policy in your store, and you were the one who waited on her when she bought the dress.

   A. Politely ask what was wrong, and point out the refund policy. Indicate that there's nothing that you can do.

   B. Recognize that "the customer is always right" and offer her another product in exchange.

   C. Listen to what she has to say, and hearing that she's feeling insecure about the way she looks, try to let her know that she looks fine wearing the article of clothing. If she's still upset, then offer her another product in exchange.

3. You realize that you don't actually like working with customers face-to-face but you still think you'd like to be in a sales business. Which of these options would you pick?

   A. Ignore your dislike of working with customers face-to-face and open a store anyway. Maybe you'll be able to hire help in the future.

   B. Decide that you can sell just as well from a Website. You don't need a store.

   C. Go into business with a friend who likes working with people and will let you take care of the other aspects of the business.

4. A service business

   A. Provides products to consumers.

   B. Often requires certain types of licenses.

   C. Provides technical expertise to customers.

5. Franchises are available

    A. In the retail and service industries.

    B. In just the retail industry.

    C. In the retail, service, and manufacturing industries.

    D. In every industry.

6. You like to sell and negotiate prices but you don't like dealing with the public. Which type of business would offer you the best fit?

    A. Manufacturing

    B. Wholesale

    C. Retail

    D. Service

7. The service industry is the largest industry in the United States.

    A. True

    B. False

8. Which is the fastest-growing industry in the United States?

    A. Child daycare services.

    B. Home healthcare services.

    C. Management, scientific, and technical consulting services.

    D. Computer-systems design and related services.

9. Industries in the United States are classified according to

    A. NAICS

    B. NCAIS

    C. OCS

    D. NCIS

10. Small businesses are the fastest growing segment of our economy. Small businesses can be in

    A. Manufacturing

    B. Retail

    C. Service

    D. All categories

Evaluation

For each of the questions, circle the number that corresponds to the letter you chose as your answer. For example, on Question 1 if you had circled "A" as your answer, then you would circle "0" opposite Question 1 and below "A."

When you have finished, add up your total and write it on the last line of the grid.

Section 3.1	Your Answer A	Your Answer B	Your Answer C	Your Answer D
Question 1	0	2	2	3
Question 2	1	3	2	--
Question 3	1	3	2	--
Question 4	0	2	2	--
Question 5	3	1	0	0
Question 6	2	3	1	0
Question 7	1	0	--	--
Question 8	0	0	3	0
Question 9	2	0	0	0
Question 10	1	1	1	3
Totals				
Total for Assessment 3.1 _____				

If Your Total Was 18 or More

You have an excellent understanding of the different types of businesses and the trends in business development. You also understand some of the qualities that are necessary for success in different sectors.

If Your Total Was 8 to 17

You have a fairly good understanding of the different types of businesses. You may want to reread certain sections of the chapter to make sure you clearly understand all the differences.

If Your Total Was 7 or Less

Recognizing the differences between types of businesses can be difficult. It might be a good idea to go through the chapter one more time and then retake the assessment.

Name _____ Class_____ Date _____

 Working on Your Business Plan

What type of business will I start?

1. Based on what you know about the different types of businesses, which is the most likely type of business you will start? *(Check one.)*

   ☐ Manufacturing

   ☐ Wholesaling

   ☐ Retailing

   ☐ Service

2. Why are you choosing this type of business?

   _____

   _____

   _____

   _____

   _____

   _____

   _____

   _____

   _____

   _____

   _____

   _____

   _____

   _____

   _____

   _____

BUSINESS PLAN PROJECT 3.1

Name _____ Class_____ Date _____

Types of Business Ownership

You've learned about the various types of business ownership. The following questions will give you an idea of how you feel about each one.

For each question, circle the answer that best represents how you think. In some cases, several may seem very close, but choose just one.

1. You've decided to go into business baking and selling brownies. You're going to have several varieties—plain brownies, brownies with icing, and your best-seller, brownies with nuts. You plan on labeling all your brownies carefully, but you're still a bit worried due to the allergies that many people have to nuts. To protect yourself, which type of business would you form?

   A. A sole proprietorship

   B. A Limited Liability Company

   C. A Subchapter S Corporation

   D. A Limited Partnership

2. You and two friends have been working together mowing lawns and you think you can expand your business to other neighborhoods if you buy more equipment. It's time to set up a legal structure. You've been working informally just as friends. What's the first thing you should do?

   A. Look for ways to get money to buy more equipment

   B. Write a partnership agreement for the three of you

   C. Pick a name for your business

3. You like having full control of your business and making all the decisions. You're willing to take any potential loss as long as you get all of the profits. You don't like filling out paperwork. What type of business structure would be best for you?

   A. A Limited Liability Company

   B. A sole proprietorship

   C. A Subchapter S Corporation

   D. Either A or C

4. Your business has done exceptionally well financially and you're ready to distribute the profits. If you have to distribute the profits as dividends to stockholders, what kind of business do you have?

   A. A nonprofit corporation.

   B. A C Corporation.

   C. A Subchapter S corporation.

   D. A sole proprietorship.

5. If you have employees in your business, you need to have

   A. A Social Security number.

   B. An employee identification number.

   C. An NAICS number.

6. In a partnership, all partners share profits, liabilities, and work loads equally.

   A. True

   B. False

7. If you have a sole proprietorship, how many employees can you have?

   A. 0

   B. 1-5

   C. 6 to 10

   D. Any number needed

8. You're thinking about forming a corporation where you're willing to give employees shares of stock as part of their compensation. Reasons for doing this are

   A. Everyone shares in the success of the company and will work harder.

   B. Everyone shares in the potential liability of the company.

   C. You will still control the management no matter how many shares you give to employees.

9. All museums are non-profit organizations.

   A. True

   B. False

10. You and your friends want to get your food and household goods at the lowest possible price. You've decided to form a cooperative. A cooperative cannot be

    A. A sole proprietorship

    B. A corporation

    C. A partnership

    D. A non-profit

Evaluation

For each of the questions, circle the number that corresponds to the letter you chose as your answer. For example, on Question 1 if you had circled "A" as your answer, then you would circle "0" opposite Question 1 and below "A."

When you have finished, add up your total and write it on the last line of the grid.

Section 3.2	Your Answer A	Your Answer B	Your Answer C	Your Answer D
Question 1	0	2	2	1
Question 2	0	3	0	--
Question 3	0	3	0	0
Question 4	0	2	2	0
Question 5	0	2	0	--
Question 6	0	1	--	--
Question 7	1	1	1	3
Question 8	3	0	2	--
Question 9	0	1	--	--
Question 10	3	0	0	0
Totals				
Total for Assessment 3.2 _____				

If Your Total Was 16 or More
You have an excellent understanding of the types of business ownership and the pros and cons of each. You·should be able to pick the right type of business for your enterprise without any problem.

If Your Total Was 8 to 15
You have a good understanding of the types of business ownership. You may want to spend a bit more time going over the advantages and disadvantages of each type so you'll be able to pick the right one for your business.

If Your Total Was 7 or Less
Understanding the differences between the various types of business ownership is essential if you plan to go into business for yourself. You want to be able to choose the right type for your own business. You may want to go over this chapter another time and pay particular attention to the various types of business ownership and the advantages and disadvantages of each.

Name _____ Class_____ Date _____

 Working on Your Business Plan

What type of business ownership is right for me?

1. Based on what you know about the different types of business ownership, which is the most likely type of business ownership for your business? *(Check one.)*

   ☐ Sole Proprietorship

   ☐ Partnership

   ☐ C Corporation

   ☐ Subchapter S Corporation

   ☐ Limited Liability Company

   ☐ Cooperative

   ☐ Nonprofit Corporation

2. Why does this form of ownership make the most sense for your business?

   _____

   _____

   _____

   _____

   _____

   _____

   _____

   _____

   _____

   _____

   _____

   _____

   _____

   _____

BUSINESS PLAN PROJECT 3.2

BUSINESS PLAN PROJECT
Section 4.1

Communicating in Business

Communication is something that all of us do every day. Effective business communication often determines the success of a project. As you answer the following questions, you'll have an idea of how much you may already know about business communication.

For each question, circle the answer that best represents how you think. In some cases, several may seem very close, but choose just one.

1. To be effective, business communications should

   A. Let the recipient know what's needed.

   B. Provide relevant information.

   C. Be courteous.

   D. All of the above

2. Giving speeches or presentations is a way of communicating orally. The best presentations are those that don't allow time for questions

   A. True

   B. False

3. All written business communications should be

   A. As easy to read as possible.

   B. As formal as possible.

   C. As brief as possible.

   D. As personal as possible.

4. Robert's construction business depends on getting payment at various stages in order to buy the materials he needs to do a project. What would be the best way for him to confirm the final arrangements for the work he's going to do with a client?

   A. In a conversation, person to person.

   B. In a telephone call.

   C. With an e-mail.

   D. With a business letter.

5. Using emoticons, such as a smiley face :) or a wink ;-) in a business communication

   A. Shows that you're a professional.

   B. Shows that you're unprofessional.

   C. Shows that you know how to have fun in your communications.

BUSINESS PLAN PROJECT 4.1

6. A good policy when making a business telephone call is to

   A. Wait until you have the right person on the phone before giving your name.

   B. Ask if the person has time to speak.

   C. Hang up if you're put on hold. You can always call later.

   D. Multi-task by doing several other things while you're talking.

7. "Keep it short and simple" is the key to effective business communication.

   A. True

   B. False

8. Before you send a business e-mail, you should

   A. Write it off-line first.

   B. Make sure the recipient can accept attachments.

   C. Go over the grammar and spelling.

   D. All of the above

9. The most important part of communicating verbally is

   A. Speaking

   B. Listening

   C. Both are equal

10. Providing feedback means that you are

   A. Telling the speaker that you understand what he/she said.

   B. Telling the speaker that you disagree with what he/she said.

   C. Telling the speaker that you agree with what he/she said.

   D. Telling the speaker what a good job he/she did.

BUSINESS PLAN PROJECT 4.1

Evaluation

For each of the questions, circle the number that corresponds to the letter you chose as your answer. For example, on Question 1 if you had circled "A" as your answer, then you would circle "1" opposite Question 1 and below "A."

When you have finished, add up your total and write it on the last line of the grid.

Section 4.1	Your Answer A	Your Answer B	Your Answer C	Your Answer D
Question 1	1	1	1	3
Question 2	0	1	--	--
Question 3	2	0	2	0
Question 4	0	0	1	3
Question 5	0	2	0	--
Question 6	0	3	0	0
Question 7	1	0	--	--
Question 8	1	1	1	3
Question 9	0	2	2	--
Question 10	3	0	0	0
Totals				
Total for Assessment 4.1 _____				

If Your Total Was 16 or More

You already know a great deal about business communication and what is appropriate in the business world. You should have no problems communicating in your business venture.

If Your Total Was 8 to 15

You have a good understanding of the requirements of business communication and how it differs from personal communication. As you read the chapter, you'll learn more information about all types of business communication.

If Your Total Was 7 or Less

Business communication is different from personal communication and it can be difficult to understand these differences at first. As you read this chapter, you'll find out almost everything you need to know about effective business communication.

Name _____ Class _____ Date _____

 Working on Your Business Plan

Continue working on your business plan. This information you provide will be used to develop an early section of your business plan.

1. Think how you would communicate what your business does. What sort of motto or slogan would you write for your business?

_____

_____

_____

_____

_____

_____

_____

_____

2. What kinds of information would you put on your business card?

_____

_____

_____

_____

_____

_____

_____

_____

_____

_____

BUSINESS PLAN PROJECT
Section 4.2

Negotiating

Negotiation takes place when people solve a problem through communication. As you answer the following questions, you'll have an idea of how you would handle different situations that require negotiation.

For each question, circle the answer that best represents how you think. In some cases, several may seem very close, but choose just one.

1. Jamar's lease is about to expire and he wants to renew it. However, he doesn't want to pay the increase that the landlord is asking. He's noticed that there are several empty spaces in his building and he thinks that the landlord may be willing to negotiate the rent. Before he speaks to the landlord, Jamar should

   A. Figure out what he'll do if the landlord isn't willing to negotiate the rent.

   B. Figure out how much money the landlord would lose if Jamar's space is vacant for a few months and be ready to point that out to the landlord in the negotiations.

   C. Think about whether he's willing to move into smaller space in the same building for the rent he's now paying.

   D. All of the above

2. Bargaining in good faith means

   A. Each party wants to get the best deal for his/her side regardless of what it means to solving the problem.

   B. Each party is willing to compromise one or two items in his/her list of demands.

   C. Each party sees the other as a partner in finding a solution.

   D. Each party believes in being completely honest.

3. Concessions are

   A. Something that you're willing to give up.

   B. Something that the other party is willing to give up.

   C. Both A and B

   D. Neither A nor B

4. You have the possibility of a new business supplier. However, she's from a country that you know little about. Before you have your first meeting, should you

   A. Just relax and figure she's doing business with you. There's nothing to worry about.

   B. Find out as much as you can about her culture and country before meeting, possibly talking to someone who has lived and worked in that country.

   C. Take the initiative and send the type of contract you usually use with suppliers before you meet, assuming you'll both sign it at the first meeting if everything goes well.

5. Negotiation in business is something that happens

    A. Frequently

    B. Occasionally

    C. Rarely

    D. Very rarely

6. When you're in negotiations, body language can be just as important to the negotiations as what is actually being said.

    A. True

    B. False

7. When negotiating with someone from a different country, it's important to

    A. Know who has the decision-making authority.

    B. Know whether they have the same attitude about time and agreements.

    C. Show respect.

    D. All of the above

8. Before you go into a negotiation, you should

    A. Be willing to state what you want.

    B. Know the differences between what you need and what you want.

    C. Be willing to make compromises.

    D. All of the above

9. A negotiation is considered successful if

    A. You get exactly what you want and the other party doesn't.

    B. You don't get exactly what you want but the other party does.

    C. An agreement is reached where both parties get what they need.

    D. An agreement is reached but the project doesn't go forward.

10. Negotiations can take place

    A. In a matter of minutes.

    B. Over several hours.

    C. Over several days.

    D. Over any amount of time.

BUSINESS PLAN PROJECT 4.2

Evaluation

For each of the questions, circle the number that corresponds to the letter you chose as your answer. For example, on Question 1 if you had circled "A" as your answer, then you would circle "1" opposite Question 1 and below "A."

When you have finished, add up your total and write it on the last line of the grid.

Section 4.2	Your Answer A	Your Answer B	Your Answer C	Your Answer D
Question 1	1	1	1	3
Question 2	0	1	2	0
Question 3	1	1	2	0
Question 4	0	3	0	--
Question 5	3	0	0	0
Question 6	1	0	--	--
Question 7	1	1	1	3
Question 8	1	1	1	3
Question 9	0	0	2	0
Question 10	1	1	1	3
Totals				
Total for Assessment 4.2 _____				

If Your Total Was 18 or More

You have an excellent understanding of negotiation and the techniques involved in conducting them. You also recognize cultural differences when negotiating. You're well on your way to becoming a successful entrepreneur!

If Your Total Was 8 to 17

You have a good understanding of negotiation and what it involves. You may want to review parts of this chapter dealing with those sections where you had some problems answering the questions. Knowing how to negotiate is essential to your future business career, no matter what you do.

If Your Total Was 7 or Less

Being able to negotiate is essential when you go into business for yourself. It's also very important in many of the dealings you'll have throughout your life. Go through the chapter one more time, paying attention to what negotiation involves, the guidelines for productive negotiations, and how to negotiate with people from other cultures. Then, retake the assessment.

Name _____ Class _____ Date _____

How ethics affect various issues and actions is an essential part of business life. As you answer the following questions, you'll get an idea of your understanding of business ethics.

For each question, circle the answer that best represents how you think. In some cases, several may seem very close, but choose just one.

1. Whether an action is ethical is always clear-cut

   A. True

   B. False

2. Universal values include

   A. Obeying the law.

   B. Not killing other people.

   C. Caring for the young and the old.

   D. All of the above

3. A company is being transparent when

   A. Everyone knows what everyone else is being paid.

   B. It communicates what it is doing and why to its employees.

   C. It uses all means of communications, including blogs and message boards, to inform employees about what it is doing and why.

   D. All of the above

4. Ashley has a dog-walking business. She often suggests to owners the best type of leash to buy for the dogs. One of her friends, Vanessa, has decided to make leashes. Vanessa asks Ashley to recommend her leashes to all her clients. Vanessa is willing to give Ashley a percentage of any sales. Vanessa's leashes are not as good as the ones Ashley currently recommends. Does Ashley face a conflict of interest if she tells her clients to buy Vanessa's leashes?

   A. Yes

   B. Possibly

   C. No

5. Intellectual property includes

   A. Copyrights

   B. Patents

   C. Trademarks

   D. All of the above

6. In order to promote ethical behavior, businesses should

   A. Protect whistle-blowers.

   B. Promote transparency.

   C. Both A and B

   D. Neither A nor B

7. When you download copyrighted materials from the Internet, make copies and give them to your customers, you are

   A. Infringing the copyright.

   B. Acting ethically.

   C. Helping to promote your business.

8. Releasing confidential information is often

   A. Unethical.

   B. Illegal.

   C. Sometimes both unethical and illegal.

   D. Never unethical or illegal.

9. All companies are required by law to have a code of ethics.

   A. True

   B. False

10. Two companies, A and B, are competing to get your business. A's prices are higher than B's, but B's reputation is a little suspect. B's company doesn't always do things strictly according to the law. As an ethical and practical businessperson, are you

    A. More likely to give your business to A, even though it will cost you more?

    B. More likely to give your business to B, despite B's reputation and pass the savings onto your customers?

    C. More likely to look for another supplier?

BUSINESS PLAN PROJECT 5.1

Evaluation

For each of the questions, circle the number that corresponds to the letter you chose as your answer. For example, on Question 1 if you had circled "A" as your answer, then you would circle "0" opposite Question 1 and below "A."

When you have finished, add up your total and write it on the last line of the grid.

Section 5.1	Your Answer A	Your Answer B	Your Answer C	Your Answer D
Question 1	0	1	--	--
Question 2	1	1	1	3
Question 3	0	2	3	0
Question 4	2	0	0	--
Question 5	1	1	1	3
Question 6	1	1	2	0
Question 7	0	1	--	--
Question 8	2	2	3	0
Question 9	0	1	--	--
Question 10	2	0	2	--
Totals				
Total for Assessment 5.1 _____				

If Your Total Was 18 or More

You have an excellent understanding of ethical business behavior and what's involved in creating an ethical workplace. This knowledge is important whether you start your own business or work for someone else.

If Your Total Was 8 to 17

You have a good understanding of ethical business behavior and what it involves. You may want to review the parts of this chapter that deal with those sections where you had some problems with the questions. Understanding and finding solutions to the ethical problems you may face in the future will be important in your future career.

If Your Total Was 7 or Less

Understanding ethical business behavior and what it involves will be necessary when you start working, whether it's for yourself or someone else. By knowing the pitfalls, you can avoid all types of problems, including legal ones that could seriously affect your business. Go through the chapter one more time, and then retake the assessment.

BUSINESS PLAN PROJECT
Section 5.2

Socially Responsible Business & Philanthropy

Acting responsibly is important to all of us as individuals. It's also important in the business world. As you answer the following questions, you'll have an idea of what you think acting responsibly means in business.

For each question, circle the answer that best represents how you think. In some cases, several may seem very close, but choose just one.

1. "Caveat emptor" means "Let the buyer beware" and is a saying from ancient Roman times. Is it a motto that a socially responsible company of today would adopt?

   A. Yes

   B. No

2. Corporations are being socially responsible when they

   A. Provide jobs for as many people as they can without worrying about profits.

   B. Buy from suppliers who offer the best prices.

   C. Balance the way they do business with the needs of society both today and in the future.

3. Bill has a service business where he goes to clients' homes. Is he showing respect towards his customers when he

   A. Doesn't use voice mail?

   B. Shows up on time?

   C. Has to come back a second time with the "right" equipment?

   D. Answers his phone when he's with another client?

4. Are companies that make products that are not environmentally friendly socially responsible?

   A. Yes

   B. Possibly

   C. No

5. "Going green" means a company is interested in

   A. Relying on coal and oil for energy.

   B. Recycling.

   C. Protecting the environment.

   D. All of the above

BUSINESS PLAN PROJECT 5.2

6. Bill wants to help his community through his business. He can

    A. Buy uniforms for a local Little League Team and put his company's name on them.

    B. Contribute a percentage of every purchase to a particular cause.

    C. Both A and B

    D. Neither A or B

7. Miguel wants to make his business energy-efficient because

    A. He cares about the environment and doesn't care how much it costs to become energy-efficient.

    B. He cares about the environment and realizes he can save money by becoming energy-efficient.

    C. It's a way to attract more customers.

8. Entrepreneurs who volunteer are making a wise investment because

    A. It helps them build professional and personal relationships.

    B. It can give them information on what may be needed in their communities.

    C. It can give them a break from worrying about their business.

    D. None of the above

9. Government standards help protect the environment.

    A. True

    B. False

10. Corporate social responsibility affects

    A. Everyone.

    B. Employees and customers of the company.

    C. Employees, customers, and suppliers of the company.

    D. Employees, customers, suppliers, investors, and creditors of the company.

BUSINESS PLAN PROJECT 5.2

Name _____ Class _____ Date _____

Evaluation

For each of the questions, circle the number that corresponds to the letter you chose as your answer. For example, on Question 1 if you had circled "A" as your answer, then you would circle "0" opposite Question 1 and below "A."

When you have finished, add up your total and write it on the last line of the grid.

Section 5.2	Your Answer A	Your Answer B	Your Answer C	Your Answer D
Question 1	0	1	--	--
Question 2	0	0	2	--
Question 3	0	3	0	0
Question 4	0	2	2	--
Question 5	0	2	2	0
Question 6	1	1	2	0
Question 7	1	2	1	--
Question 8	1	1	1	0
Question 9	1	0	--	--
Question 10	3	1	1	2
Totals				
Total for Assessment 5.2 _____				

If Your Total Was 14 or More

You have an excellent understanding of what corporate social responsibility entails. You realize that it includes responsibility to individuals and the community as well as the environment. This knowledge is important whether you start your own business or work for someone else.

If Your Total Was 8 to 13

You have a good understanding of corporate social responsibility and what it involves. When businesses act in ways that balance profit and growth with the good of society, everyone benefits.

If Your Total Was 7 or Less

Understanding corporate social responsibility can be difficult at first, but you'll soon learn what it involves. Corporate social responsibility helps businesses treat everyone ethically. It also helps businesses give back to the community and protect the environment.

Name _____ Class _____ Date _____

 Working on Your Business Plan

How is my business socially responsible?

1. How would you use cause-related marketing in your business?

_____

_____

_____

_____

_____

_____

_____

_____

_____

_____

2. Describe how your company will be socially responsible.

_____

_____

_____

_____

_____

_____

_____

_____

_____

_____

_____

BUSINESS PLAN PROJECT
Section 6.1

What Is a Business Plan?

You are ready to begin developing a business plan for your own business!

The outline for your business plan is shown below. You will be filling in your business plan section-by-section as you work through this Business Plan Project. You can use the Business Plan Template provided at the end of this Workbook (beginning on page 363). Alternatively, you could use the Microsoft Word format of the Business Plan Template available on the Student Center at entrepreneurship.pearson.com. BizTech also uses this Business Plan Template.

You won't develop your Executive Summary until after you have written the entire business plan.

BUSINESS PLAN

1. BUSINESS IDEA

1.1   Qualifications

1.2   Factors Influencing Demand

1.3   Type of Business

1.4   Type of Business Ownership

1.5   Social Responsibility

2. OPPORTUNITY & MARKET ANALYSIS

2.1   Business Opportunity

2.2   Market Research

2.3   Competitors

2.4   Competitive Advantage

2.5   Marketing Plan

2.6   Pricing Strategy

2.7   Promotion

2.8   Sales Methods

3. FINANCIAL STRATEGIES

3.1   Sales Estimates

3.2   Business Costs

3.4   Income Statement

3.5   Balance Sheet

3.6   Financial Ratios

3.7   Break-Even Point

3.8   Financing Strategy

3.9   Recordkeeping & Accounting Systems

4.   ORGANIZATIONAL STRUCTURES

4.1   Organizational Structure

4.2   Staffing

4.3   Outside Experts

4.4   Training and Motivating Employees

5.   LEGAL STRUCTURES

5.1   Intellectual Property

5.2   Contracts

5.3   Insurance

5.4   Taxes

5.5   Government Regulations

6.   BUSINESS MANAGEMENT

6.1   Expenses, Credit, and Cash Flow

6.2   Production and Distribution

6.3   Operations

6.4   Purchasing

6.5   Inventory

7.   PLAN FOR GROWTH

7.1   Business Growth

7.2   Challenges

7.3   Franchising and Licensing

7.4   Exit Strategy

Name _____ Class_____ Date _____

Begin Filling in Your Business Plan

If you've completed the previous sections of the Business Plan Project, you've already begun doing some work on your business plan. You can begin filling in your Business Plan now.

1. **Refer to page 231 of this** *Business Plan Project.* You wrote down a name for your business. Now, at the top of your business plan, write that name under "BUSINESS PLAN."

2. **Refer to pages 231 and 232 of this** *Business Plan Project.* You described your academic and work qualifications related to your new business. You also checked off your strongest entrepreneurial characteristics. Now write down your qualifications under Section 1.1 ("Qualifications") of your business plan. Then describe your personal characteristics and skills. Make sure to mention the three entrepreneurial characteristics you checked off.

3. **Refer to page 236 of this** *Business Plan Project.* You wrote down the factors that will influence demand for your product or service. Write these factors under Section 1.2 ("Factors Influencing Demand") of your business plan.

4. **Refer to page 243 of this** *Business Plan Project.* You checked off the type of business you will start. You also wrote your reasons for choosing this type of business. Under Section 1.3 ("Type of Business"), write down the type of business you will start and your primary reason for choosing this type of business.

5. **Refer to page 247 of this** *Business Plan Project.* You checked off the type of business ownership you will use for your new business. You also described why this type of ownership made the most sense for your business. Under Section 1.4 ("Type of Business Ownership"), write down the type of business ownership you will use for your company. Then write downs you primary reason for choosing this type of business ownership.

6. **Refer to page 251 of this** *Business Plan Project.* You wrote a slogan or motto for your business. Write the slogan or motto under your business name at the top of your business plan

7. **Refer to page 261 of this** *Business Plan Project.* You described how your business would be socially responsible, including whether it would use cause-related marketing. Under Section 1.5 ("Social Responsibility"), write down your plan for making your company socially responsible. Include any plans you may have for cause-related marketing.

Take a minute to look at what you've done so far. You've filled in information under sections 1.1 through 1.5 of your business plan. Take the time now to write the information in your business plan more formally. See Eva's business plan on page 195 of your textbook as a model.

As you continue to develop your business plan, you will probably need to revise these sections a few times. That's normal. That's why it's a good idea to develop your business plan using word-processing software. It allows you to make changes more easily.

Name _____ Class_____ Date _____

Is my idea for a business a real business opportunity?

SWOT Analysis

Complete a SWOT analysis for your business opportunity.

Type of Business

1. What type of business are you planning?

_____

Strengths

2. What skills do you have that would enable you to do well with this specific opportunity? What resources do you have available (time, money, and people who can help you)? Do you have any unique knowledge or experience that could give you an edge?

_____

_____

_____

_____

_____

_____

Weaknesses

3. In what skill or knowledge areas do you need to improve? What resources are you lacking? What might potential customers see as a weakness in your product or service?

_____

_____

_____

_____

_____

_____

Opportunities

4. Does this business idea fill an unmet need or want? Are there any trends or changes happening in your community that you could use as an advantage? What could you do better than other companies that are already in the same type of business? Does the proposed business location give you any advantages?

_____

_____

_____

_____

_____

_____

_____

Threats

5. What obstacles stand in the way of pursuing this opportunity? What current trends could potentially harm your business? How fierce is the competition in this business area? Does this business idea have a short window of opportunity?

_____

_____

_____

_____

_____

_____

_____

Business Opportunity

Use the information from your SWOT analysis to write Section 2.1 ("Business Opportunity") of your business plan. Use Eva's business plan (on pages 196 and 197) as a model.

Consider using charts or diagrams in your description.

If you want to, you can include the completed SWOT Analysis in your business plan.

BUSINESS PLAN PROJECT
Section 7.1

What Is Market Research?

Conducting Market Research

How should I conduct market research?

Read more about the six steps in researching a market in Section 7.2 of your textbook.

Identify Research Objectives

1. What are your research objectives? What information do you need? What problems are you trying to solve?

   a. List your research objectives related to the industry.

   _____

   _____

   _____

   _____

   _____

   b. List your research objectives related to your targeted customers.

   _____

   _____

   _____

   _____

   _____

   c. List your research objectives related to your competition. *(You will research your competition in Section 7.2.)*

   _____

   _____

   _____

   _____

   _____

   _____

BUSINESS PLAN PROJECT 7.1

Determine Methods and Sources

2. Based on your objectives, decide which research methods will best help you achieve your goals.

    a. Will you use secondary data sources such as:

    ☐ Government Sources *(Describe)*

_____

_____

    ☐ Trade Groups and Journals *(Describe)*

_____

_____

    ☐ Business Magazines and Reports *(Describe)*

_____

_____

    ☐ Local Community Resources *(Describe)*

_____

_____

    b. Will you use primary data sources such as:

    ☐ Interviews/Surveys *(Describe)*

_____

_____

    ☐ Focus Groups *(Describe)*

_____

_____

    ☐ Observations *(Describe)*

_____

_____

Gather the Data

3. Now conduct market research related to your industry and your customer. You will research your competition in Section 7.2.

Organize the Data

4. Group and organize data as you gather it. Keep careful records of your secondary data sources.

Analyze the Data

5. Consider developing charts, graphs, tables, or diagrams to help you analyze your data visually.

Draw Conclusions

6. When you have analyzed your market research on the industry and the market, continue to the next step.

 Target Market

7. Based on your research, describe the total market for your product or service and your market segment.

_____

_____

_____

_____

_____

_____

8. Now, within your market segment, describe your target market. Be as detailed as you can.

_____

_____

_____

_____

_____

_____

Use these descriptions to write Section 2.2 ("Market Research") of your business plan. Use Eva's business plan (on page 197) as a model. Consider using charts or diagrams in your description. Make sure to cite secondary data sources accurately and correctly.

BUSINESS PLAN PROJECT 7.1

BUSINESS PLAN PROJECT
Section 7.2

What Is Your Competitive Advantage?

Who are my competitors?
What is my competitive advantage?

Competitors

1. Research the competition, both direct and indirect, for your business. (Use secondary and primary sources, as appropriate.)

2. Identify your direct competition. (Fill in the competitor information below.)

Competitor Name	Address	Phone	Website/E-Mail

3. Describe your *direct* competition.

_____

_____

_____

_____

_____

_____

_____

_____

_____

_____

Name _____ Class_____ Date _____

4. Describe your *indirect* competition.

_____

_____

_____

_____

_____

_____

_____

_____

Competitive Advantage

Identify your competitive advantage.

5. Fill out the following Competitive Matrix to help identify your competitive advantages.

Factors	Your Business	Competitor A	Competitor B	Competitor C
Price				
Quality of Product/ Service				
Location				
Reputation/Brands				
Delivery Method				
Customer Service				
Unique Factors and Knowledge				

If you don't have data about some aspect of your competitor to fill in the competitive matrix, then do additional research to fill in the matrix completely.

6. Ask yourself these four questions to help identify potential differentiators for your business:

- What product or service can your business provide that your competitors don't?

- What mix of products or services can your business provide that your competitors don't?

- What specialized selling or delivery method can give your business a competitive edge?

- In what unique ways can your business meet customers' wants or needs?

Name _____ Class _____ Date _____

Based on your differentiators, describe your competitive advantages. *(Try to identify at least three competitive advantages.)*

a. _____

_____

b. _____

_____

c. _____

_____

d. _____

_____

e. _____

_____

7. Expand your SWOT Analysis to show your business compared to your direct competitors.

Business	Strengths	Weaknesses	Opportunities	Threats
Your Business				
Competitor A				
Competitor B				
Competitor C				

Competitors

Use the information from above to write Section 2.2 ("Competition") of your business plan. Use Eva's business plan (on page 197) as a model. Discuss direct competition and indirect competition separately.

Competitive Advantage

Use the information from above to write Section 2.3 ("Competitive Advantage") of your business plan. Use Eva's business plan (on page 198) as a model.

BUSINESS PLAN PROJECT 7.2

BUSINESS PLAN PROJECT
Section 8.1

Developing Your Marketing Mix

What is my marketing plan?
What are my product and pricing strategies?

Setting Marketing Goals

Set Short-Range Goals

1. What do you want to accomplish over the next year? *Breaking your short-range goals down into quarters (3-month periods) is often helpful.*

   a. List your goals for the next quarter (the next three months).

   _____

   _____

   _____

   _____

   b. List your goals for the quarter after that.

   _____

   _____

   _____

   _____

   c. List your goals for the quarter after that.

   _____

   _____

   _____

   _____

   d. List your goals for the quarter after that.

   _____

   _____

   _____

   _____

Describe Mid-Range Goals

2. Describe what you want to achieve in your business in the next two to five years.

_____

_____

_____

_____

Describe Long-Range Goals

3. Where do you see your business ten or twenty years from now?

_____

_____

_____

_____

Marketing Plan

A marketing plan focuses on the Five P's: People, Product, Place, Price, and Promotion. You will now focus on the people, product, place, and price portions of the marketing plan. You will focus on Promotion in the next section of this Business Plan Project.

People Strategies

4. Who is your target customer? Provide a detailed profile of your target.

_____

_____

_____

_____

_____

_____

_____

_____

_____

Name _____ Class_____ Date _____

Product Strategies

5. Will you sell more than one product or service?

☐ **Yes**   ☐ **No**

If **Yes**, describe your product/service mix. *(This is often described on a percentage basis, for example: 60% of Product A and 40% of Product B.)* Then describe your most significant products/services in detail.

Product/Service Mix: _____

_____

_____

Most Significant Products/Services: _____

_____

_____

_____

_____

If **No**, describe your product or service in detail.

_____

_____

_____

_____

6. Now, describe the features and benefits of your product/service. List at least three benefits of your product or service. *(Remember that a feature is what the product or service does and how it appears to the senses. A benefit is the reason a customer chooses to buy your product. Every product benefit is a result of a feature.)*

Feature	Benefit
1.	
2.	
3.	
4.	
5.	
6.	

7. Will you create a brand for your product or service?

☐ **Yes**   ☐ **No**

If **Yes**, describe your branding strategy and, if you are using a brand mark, include it.

_____

_____

_____

_____

_____

8. If you are selling a product, how will it be packaged? Describe your packaging in detail.

_____

_____

_____

_____

Place Strategies

9. If you are selling a product, what channel of distribution will you use? Describe your channel of distribution *(that is, the way in which your product will reach the ultimate consumer).*

_____

_____

_____

_____

10. Where will you sell your product or service? Describe where you will sell your product or service. Also, include the hours during which the customer can buy it.

_____

_____

_____

_____

_____

BUSINESS PLAN PROJECT 8.1

Will you need to transport your product?

☐ **Yes**   ☐ **No**

If **Yes**, describe the method you will use to transport your product. Also describe the type of shipping container you will need.

Method of Transport: _____

_____

Shipping Container: _____

_____

Price Strategies

11. What is your price objective? Describe what you want to achieve with your price. *(Some examples of price objectives are: maximizing profits, obtaining market share, increasing sales volume, or building an image. See page 219 of your textbook for help in identifying price objectives.)*

_____

_____

_____

_____

12. What strategy for determining prices will you use? Pick one. *(These are discussed on pages 219–220 in your textbook.)*

☐ Demand-Based Pricing (Focuses on how much customers are willing to pay)

☐ Competition-Based Pricing (Focuses on what the competition charges)

☐ Cost-Based Pricing (Focuses on how much it costs your business to provide the product or service)

Will your business sell products?

☐ **Yes**   ☐ **No**

If **Yes**, describe your pricing structure:

_____

_____

_____

If you are selling a product, will you use an indirect channel of distribution?

☐ **Yes**   ☐ **No**

If **Yes**, have you allowed for the appropriate markup in price? *(The price will get adjusted as it moves through the channel of distribution.)* Describe the markups that will apply to your product as it moves through the channel of distribution. Also indicate what you expect the ultimate price to the customer will be.

_____

_____

_____

_____

_____

13. Will your business be selling services?

☐ **Yes**   ☐ **No**

If **Yes**, how will you price your services? Pick one:

☐ By Time (You could charge by the hour, by 15-minute periods, or even by the minute.) Describe how you will price your time:

_____

_____

_____

☐ By Time and Materials (You could charge by the hour, by 15-minute periods, or even by the minute. You will charge separately per job for any materials used.) Describe how you will price your time and your materials:

_____

_____

_____

☐ Flat Rate (This includes a specific service, including any materials, for one flat rate.) Describe your rate:

_____

_____

_____

14. Will you be bundling your products or services? *(Bundling is the practice of combining the price of several services (and/or physical products) into one price. See page 221 of the textbook for more information about bundling.)*

☐ **Yes**   ☐ **No**

If **Yes**, describe how you will be bundling your products or services.

_____

_____

_____

_____

Use the description of your Marketing Plan, above, to write Sections 2.5 ("Marketing Plan") and 2.6 ("Pricing Strategy")of your business plan. Use Eva's business plan (on page 198) as a model.

Name _____ Class_____ Date _____

Promoting Your Product

How do I promote my product?

 ## Choosing a Promotional Mix

The last of the Five P's is Promotion. That's what you will focus on in this section of the Business Plan Project.

Advertising

Advertising is a public, promotional message paid for by an identified sponsor or company.

1. Will you use print advertising (ads in newspapers, magazines, The Yellow Pages, etc.)?

   ☐ **Yes**   ☐ **No**

   If **Yes**, describe your plan for using print advertising.

   _____

   _____

   _____

   _____

   _____

   _____

   _____

   _____

   _____

   _____

   _____

   _____

   _____

   _____

   _____

2. Will you use direct-mail advertising (mailed brochures, print catalogs, fliers, postcards, sales letters, newsletters, etc.)?

☐ **Yes**   ☐ **No**

If **Yes**, describe your plan for using direct-mail advertising.

_____

_____

_____

_____

_____

_____

_____

_____

_____

_____

_____

_____

_____

_____

_____

_____

_____

_____

3. Will you use radio or television advertising?

☐ **Yes**   ☐ **No**

If **Yes**, describe your plan for using radio or television advertising.

_____

_____

_____

_____

4. Will you use Internet advertising (sending e-mails to customers, creating an electronic catalog on a Website, etc.)?

☐ **Yes**   ☐ **No**

If **Yes**, describe your plan for using Internet advertising.

_____

_____

_____

_____

_____

_____

_____

_____

_____

5. Will you use some other form of advertising (product placement, outdoor advertising, posters, banners, etc.)?

☐ **Yes**   ☐ **No**

If **Yes**, describe your plans.

_____

_____

_____

_____

BUSINESS PLAN PROJECT 8.2

Visual Merchandising

Visual merchandising is the artistic display of products to attract customers and influence them to purchase the products.

6. Will you use visual merchandising?

☐ **Yes**   ☐ **No**

If **Yes**, describe your plan for using visual merchandising.

_____

_____

_____

_____

Public Relations & Publicity

Public relations are activities aimed at creating goodwill toward a product or a company. Publicity is a form of promotion for which a company doesn't pay.

7. Will you be sending out press releases?

☐ **Yes**   ☐ **No**

If **Yes**, describe your plan for sending out press releases.

_____

_____

_____

_____

_____

_____

_____

_____

_____

_____

_____

BUSINESS PLAN PROJECT 8.2

8. Will you be sponsoring any events (community events, business events, etc.)?

☐ **Yes**   ☐ **No**

If **Yes**, describe your plan for sponsoring events.

_____

_____

_____

_____

_____

_____

_____

_____

_____

_____

9. Will you be sponsoring any contests?

☐ **Yes**   ☐ **No**

If **Yes**, describe your plan for sponsoring contests.

_____

_____

_____

_____

_____

_____

_____

_____

_____

_____

BUSINESS PLAN PROJECT 8.2

Personal Selling and Sales Promotion

Personal selling is a direct one-to-one effort to increase sales and build customer relations. Sales Promotions are short-term activities that provide a buying incentive.

10. Will you be doing personal selling?

☐ **Yes**   ☐ **No**

If **Yes**, describe your plan for personal selling. (Will you meet potential customers in person? Will you call potential customers? How will you locate potential customers?)

_____

_____

_____

_____

_____

_____

_____

_____

_____

_____

_____

11. Will you be offering any sales promotions (such as product demonstrations, coupons, free samples, sales, etc.)?

☐ **Yes**   ☐ **No**

If **Yes**, describe your plans for sales promotions.

_____

_____

_____

_____

Use the description of your Marketing Plan, above, to write Section 2.7 ("Promotion") of your business plan. Use Eva's business plan (on page 199) as a model.

Use the Table on the next page to show your promotional mix. Consider including it in your business plan.

Promotional Mix

	Street Vending	Your Office	Door-to-Door	Flea Markets	School/ Community	Local Stores	Youth Clubs	Internet	Other
Business Cards									
Posters									
Flyers									
Phone Sales									
Sales Calls									
Brochures									
Mailings									
Newspaper/ Radio/TV									
Website									
Other									

Name _____ Class _____ Date _____

Principles of Successful Selling

How do I sell my product?

Selling Your Product or Service

One of the most important elements in your promotional mix is personal selling. It helps build personal relationships and allows for customized communication.

Sales Leads
A sales lead is a person or company that has some characteristics of your target market.

1. What percentage of promotional response will you depend on for sales leads? *Promotional responses are from people who respond to your promotional efforts. For example, someone who responded because they received a flier or a postcard.*

    Indicate a percentage: _____

    List the promotional pieces that you expect will generate your sales leads.

    _____

    _____

    _____

    _____

    _____

2. What percentage of referrals will you depend on for sales leads? *When a person provides contact information for someone else who may be interested in your product or service that's a referral.*

    Indicate a percentage: _____

    Describe how you will generate referrals.

    _____

    _____

    _____

    _____

    _____

3. What percentage of data mining will you depend on for sales leads? *Data mining is the process of using a computer program to search large collections of data for contacts. In some cases you can purchase data that has already been collected.*

Indicate a percentage: _____

Describe what data sources you will used to generate sales leads.

_____

_____

_____

_____

_____

_____

4. What percentage of cold calls will you depend on for sales leads? *A cold call is when you contact someone you don't know without prior notice.*

Indicate a percentage: _____

Describe how you will select people to cold call.

_____

_____

_____

_____

_____

Overall Selling Strategy

5. What will be your overall selling strategy? Describe what you will say to a sales prospect.

_____

_____

_____

_____

_____

_____

Overcoming Objections

6. What are the most common objections in a sales call? How will you overcome them? List the three most common objections on the left. Then, on the right, describe how you intend to respond to that objection.

Objection	Response
1.	
2.	
3.	

First Prospects

7. Many times we already know people or businesses who are likely prospects. Name three prospects you will contact.

Contact 1. _____

Contact 2. _____

Contact 3. _____

Use the description of your Marketing Plan, above, to write Sections 2.8 ("Sales Methods") of your business plan. Use Eva's business plan (on page 200) as a model.

Consider using a pie chart to show how you will generate sales leads.

Name _____ Class _____ Date _____

BUSINESS PLAN PROJECT
Section 9.2

How do I estimate sales?

Sales-Forecasting Techniques

A sales estimate is a key part of your company's financial-planning process. Typically a new business is not able to base its sales estimate on past sales. Some common forecasting techniques are discussed on pages 256 through 258 of the textbook.

1. Which sales-forecasting techniques will you use to prepare your sales estimate?

   ☐ Full Capacity

   ☐ Observational Data

   ☐ Industry Standards

   ☐ Industry/Seasonal Cycles

   ☐ Team Effort

   ☐ Number of Customers versus Distance

   ☐ Market Share

   ☐ Proportional Scaling

   ☐ Other

2. Describe in detail how you will create your first-year sales estimate.

   _____

   _____

   _____

   _____

   _____

   _____

   _____

   _____

   _____

Estimating Sales for the First Two Years

3. Are there any assumptions that you are making about your first-year sales that should be included in your business plan? If so, describe them in detail.

_____

_____

_____

_____

_____

4. What will your first-year sales be? List your estimated sales *for the first year only* in the table below. Show your units and sales revenue.

Month	Year 1		Year 2	
	Units	**Sales Revenue**	**Units**	**Sales Revenue**
January				
February				
March				
April				
May				
June				
July				
August				
September				
October				
November				
December				
Annual Totals				

BUSINESS PLAN PROJECT 9.2

5. What will your sales be in your second year? *Entrepreneurs often estimate their second-year sales as some percentage of the first-year sales.*

   a. Do you think sales will decline in the second year?

      ☐ **Yes**   ☐ **No**

      If Yes, by what percentage? _____

      Why? _____

   b. Do you think sales will be flat (that is, neither increase nor decrease) in the second year?

      ☐ **Yes**   ☐ **No**

      If Yes, by what percentage? _____

      Why? _____

   c. Do you think sales will increase in the second year?

      ☐ **Yes**   ☐ **No**

      If Yes, by what percentage? _____

      Why? _____

   d. Will there be any special factors to take into consideration in regard to your second year sales?

      ☐ **Yes**   ☐ **No**

      If Yes, describe them. _____

      _____

      _____

   e. Now, enter your projected second-year sales month-by-month in the table.

Estimating Sales for Years Three Through Five

6. Are there any assumptions that you are making about your sales in your third through your fifth year of business that should be included in your business plan? If so, describe them in detail.

   _____

   _____

   _____

   _____

BUSINESS PLAN PROJECT 9.2

7. What do you estimate your sales in years 3 through 5 will be? Sales are often estimated as some percentage of the previous year's sales.

a. In Year 3, will sales:

☐ Increase? If so, by what percentage? _____

☐ Stay flat?

☐ Decrease? If so, by what percentage? _____

Will there be any special factors affecting sales in your third year? If so, describe them.

_____

b. In Year 4, will sales:

☐ Increase? If so, by what percentage? _____

☐ Stay flat?

☐ Decrease? If so, by what percentage? _____

Will there be any special factors affecting sales in your fourth year? If so, describe them.

_____

c. In Year 5, will sales:

☐ Increase? If so, by what percentage? _____

☐ Stay flat?

☐ Decrease? If so, by what percentage? _____

Will there be any special factors affecting sales in your fifth year? If so, describe them.

_____

d. Enter your projected annual sales for the first five years.

	Units	Sales Revenue
Year 1		
Year 2		
Year 3		
Year 4		
Year 5		
Five-Year Total		

Use the sales estimates to write Sections 3.1 ("Sales Estimates") of your business plan. Use Eva's business plan (on pages 200 and 201 of the textbook) as a model.

Consider using a bar chart to show your projected five-year sales (both units and sales revenue).

BUSINESS PLAN PROJECT 9.2

Name _____ Class_____ Date _____

The Cost of Doing Business

What are my business costs?

Estimating Fixed Operating Expenses

1. What are your monthly fixed operating expenses? In the following table, list your *monthly* expenses for all the categories that apply. *(For any expense that isn't monthly, calculate the monthly amount. For example, if an expense is paid every other month, you would divide it by 2.)*

Expense Category	Monthly Expense	Annual Expense
Advertising		
Depreciation		
Insurance, Auto		
Insurance, Health		
Insurance, Life		
Interest		
Rent		
Salaries		
Telephone		
Utilities		
Other:		
Other:		
Other:		

BUSINESS PLAN PROJECT 10.1

2. What are your annual fixed operating expenses? Multiply your monthly amount by 12. List your *annual* fixed expenses in the table.

3. Do you need to describe any special circumstances relating to your fixed operating expenses in the business plan? For instance, are your parents paying for certain expenses? Are you listing any unusual expenses? Are there some expenses that would normally occur but in your business are absent? Describe those circumstances here.

_____

_____

_____

_____

_____

_____

_____

_____

_____

Use this portion of the Business Plan Project to write Section 3.2 ("Business Expenses Estimates") of your business plan. Use Eva's business plan (on page 202 of the textbook) as a model.

Consider using a pie chart to show your individual operating expenses as a percentage of the annual total.

BUSINESS PLAN PROJECT
Section 10.2

The Economics of One Unit of Sale

How do I measure the economics of one unit?

Economics of One Unit of Sale

1. For your business, what is one unit of sale? *Remember that a unit of sale is what the customer actually buys from you. It's the amount of product (or service) you use to figure your operations and profit.* Describe your unit of sale.

   _____

   _____

   _____

2. What is your selling price for one unit of sale? *(You established a price for one unit of sale in Section 8.1 of this Business Plan Project.)* List your price per unit of sale.

   _____

Estimating Variable Expenses

3. What are your variable expenses per unit of sale? In the following table, list your variable expenses per unit of sale for all the categories that apply.

Expense Category	Per Unit
Labor ($____/Hour)	
Materials	
Commissions	
Shipping & Handling	
Packaging	
Other:	
Other:	
Other:	

4. Do you need to describe any special circumstances relating to your variable expenses in the business plan? For instance, what materials are used in a service business? Why is special packaging needed? Describe those circumstances here.

_____

_____

_____

 Economics of One Unit of Sale

5. What are the economics of one unit of sale for your business? Fill in the following form with your information. *(You may need to modify it to fit your type of business. See pages 276 through 282 of the textbook for various models of EOUs based on specific types of businesses.)*

ONE UNIT OF SALE = _____

SELLING PRICE (PER UNIT): $_____

    Variable Costs

        Cost of Goods

            Materials $_____

            Labor ($15 per Hour)   _____

            Cost of Goods Sold $_____

        Other Variable Costs

            Commissions $_____

            Shipping & Handling   _____

            Other Variable Costs   _____

    Total Variable Costs   _____

CONTRIBUTION MARGIN (PER UNIT): $_____

Use this portion of the Business Plan Project to write Section 3.3 ("Economics of One Unit") of your business plan. Use Eva's business plan (on page 202 of the textbook) as a model.

Consider using a pie chart to show your individual variable expenses as a percentage of the selling price.

BUSINESS PLAN PROJECT 10.2

BUSINESS PLAN PROJECT
Section 11.1

Income Statements & Cash Flow

How do I develop an income statement and track cash flow?

You will develop a projected traditional-format income statement for your business plan.

Time Period

The projected income statement in your business plan will be for a one-year period.

1. What time period will you use for your projected income statement?

   ☐ A calendar year (January 1 through December 31)

   ☐ A fiscal year running from _____

   through _____

Differences in Income Statements

Income statements for different types of businesses show the variable expenses related to the Cost of Goods or Services differently.

2. What type of business are you planning?

   ☐ Merchandising (wholesale or retail) business

   Use "Cost of Goods Sold" for your variable expenses. Merchandising companies keep track of the cost of their beginning inventory, any additional inventory they purchase, and the cost of their ending inventory. *(See pg. 293 of the textbook for an example of this type of income statement.)*

   ☐ Manufacturing business

   Use "Cost of Goods Manufactured and Sold." Manufacturing companies track the cost of labor and materials. *(See pg. 297 of the textbook for an example of this type of income statement.)*

   ☐ Service business

   Use "Cost of Services Sold." Service companies may track the materials involved in providing their services. They may also show the cost of labor if the service can easily be broken down into units. When labor is paid by the hour or costs are based on one project, you wouldn't include this section. *(See pg. 299 of the textbook for an example of this type of income statement.)*

Monthly Projected Income Statement

New business owners often find it helpful to project their annual sales and expenses for the first year of business.

3. Complete a monthly projected income statement for the first year of business *(on the next page).*

PROJECTED MONTHLY INCOME STATEMENT
First Year

	Jan.	Feb.	Mar.	Apr.	May	June	July	Aug.	Sept.	Oct.	Nov.	Dec.	**Total**
Units Sold													
Unit Selling Price													
Sales Revenue													
Cost of _____ Sold													
Gross Profit													
Total Operating Expenses													
Pre-Tax Profit													
Taxes (15%)													
Net Profit													

Here's how you fill in this form:

- "Units Sold": Use your sales estimates from Section 9.2 (page 292 of this *Business Plan Project*).

- "Unit Selling Price": Use your pricing structure from Section 8.1 (pages 278–280 of this *Business Plan Project*).

- "Sales Revenue": Multiply "Units Sold" by the "Unit Selling Price" for each month.

- "Cost of _____ Sold": Fill in the appropriate heading based on #2 "Differences in Income Statements," earlier in this Section. (For example, if your business were a service business, you would write "Cost of Services Sold.") Multiply the appropriate variable expenses by the number of units of sale for the month.

- "Gross Profit": Subtract the previous line from "Revenue: Sales."

- "Total Operating Expenses": Enter your monthly operating expenses from Section 10.1 (page 295 of this *Business Plan Project*).

- "Pre-Tax Profit": Subtract the previous line from "Gross Profit."

- "Taxes": Multiply your Pre-Tax Profit by 15% (0.15).

- "Net Profit": Subtract the previous line from "Pre-Tax Profit."

Projected Cash Flow Statement

While not part of the typical Business Plan, a Cash Flow Statement is a very important document in the first year of a business's life.

4. Will I need to buy any equipment in my first year?

   ☐ **Yes** The cost for the equipment will be: _____

   ☐ **No**

5. How much cash will I need in my first year? *Fill in the following Cash Flow Statement.*

PROJECTED CASH FLOW STATEMENT
End of First Year

BEGINNING CASH BALANCE $_____

CASH INFLOW

    Investment $_____

    Sales   _____

    Total Cash Inflow $_____

CASH OUTFLOW

    Variable Expenses (*COGS*) $_____

    Other Variable Expenses   _____

    Fixed Operating Expenses   _____

    Equipment   _____

    Other Outflows   _____

    Total Cash Outflow $_____

NET CASH FLOW $_____

Here's how you fill in this form:

- "Beginning Cash Balance": Since this is your first year in business, you probably started with no beginning cash balance.

- "Investment": Enter how much money you plan to invest in the business in its first year.

- "Sales": Use your projected annual sales revenue estimates from Section 9.2 (page 292 of this *Business Plan Project*).

- "Variable Expenses (*COGS*)": Choose the applicable title. Use your projected annual-units total from Section 9.2 (page 292 of this *Business Plan Project*). Multiply by the expense of the goods/materials.

- "Other Variable Expenses": Use the unit-variable-expense totals from Section 10.2 (page 297 of this *Business Plan Project*). Multiply by the annual-units total from Section 9.2 (page 292 of this *Business Plan Project*).

- "Fixed Operating Totals": Use the total projected annual fixed operating costs from Section 10.1 (page 295 of this *Business Plan Project).*

- "Equipment": If applicable, enter the cost of the equipment you will purchase in your first year.

- "Other Outflows": Enter any other cash outflows you project in your first year.

- "Total Cash Outflows": Enter the total of all your cash outflows.

- "Net Cash Flow": Subtract the Total Cash Outflow from the Total Cash Inflow.

If you have a positive Net Cash Flow, you are projecting that you will have enough cash for your first year. If you have a negative cash flow, you will need to increase your cash inflow (perhaps by increasing sales or seeking additional investment) or decrease your cash outflow (perhaps by reducing your expenses).

To be a successful businessperson, you will need to work on your Cash Flow Statement until you achieve a positive Net Cash Flow.

Annual Income Statement

6. How do you develop an annual income statement to include in your business plan? *Fill out the following income statement form (on the next page) and include it in your business plan.*

Here's how you fill in this form:

- "Sales Revenue": Use your total Sales Revenue from the chart earlier in this Section.

- "Cost of _____ Sold": Fill in the appropriate heading just as you did in the earlier chart in this Section. Fill in any Labor or Materials costs based on the number of units sold in a year from Section 9.2 (page 292 of this Business Plan Project) multiplied by the Labor or Materials expenses (if applicable) from Section 10.2 (page 297 of this *Business Plan Project*).

- "Gross Profit": Subtract the Cost of _____ Sold from the Sales Revenue.

- "Operating Expenses": Fill in your annual Operating Expenses from Section 10.1 (page 295 of this *Business Plan Project*).

- "Total Operating Expenses": Total all your separate Operating Expenses.

- "Pre-Tax Profit": Subtract your Total Operating Expenses from your Gross Profit.

- "Taxes": Multiply your Pre-Tax Profit by 15% (0.15).

- "Net Profit": Subtract your taxes from your Pre-Tax Profit.

Name _____ Class _____ Date _____

PROJECTED ANNUAL INCOME STATEMENT
MONTHLY INCOME STATEMENT
End of First Year

REVENUE

Sales $_____

Total Revenue $_____

COST OF _____ SOLD

Labor? _____ $_____

Materials? _____ _____

Cost of _____ Sold _____

GROSS PROFIT $_____

OPERATING EXPENSES

Advertising $_____

Depreciation _____

Insurance _____

Interest _____

Telephone _____

Utilities (Gas, Electric) _____

Other Fixed Cost (_____) _____

Other Fixed Cost (_____) _____

Other Fixed Cost (_____) _____

Other Fixed Cost (_____) _____

Total Operating Expenses _____

PRE-TAX PROFIT $_____

Taxes (15%) _____

NET PROFIT $_____

Use this portion of the Business Plan Project to complete a projected annual income statement for Section 3.4 ("Income Statement") of your business plan. Use Eva's business plan (on page 203 of the textbook) as a model.

Consider using a pie chart to show a same-size analysis of your income statement.

BUSINESS PLAN PROJECT 11.1

Name _____ Class _____ Date _____

The Balance Sheet

How do I develop a balance sheet?

Balance Sheet

Your projected balance sheet shows your Assets, Liabilities, and Owner's Equity at the end of your first Year.

1. How do you develop a projected annual balance sheet to include in your business plan? *Fill out the following balance sheet and include it in your business plan.*

   For many entries in the Balance Sheet, you will need to make your best judgment, based on your Cash Flow Statement and both monthly and annual Income Statements (all from Section 11.1 of this Business Project Plan, pages 299 to 303).

   For the balance sheet in your business plan, show only those lines on which you have made an entry.

   Remember that Assets – Liabilities = Owner's Equity.

   For Owner's Equity: The term is "Owner's Equity" only if your business is a sole proprietorship or partnership. For corporations, the appropriate term is "Shareholder's Equity." Enter your name on the blank line. Indicate the percentages of ownership for partnerships. Indicate the number of shares held by shareholders in corporations.

PROJECTED ANNUAL BALANCE SHEET
End of First Year

ASSETS

Current Assets

Cash $_____

Inventory   _____

Accounts Receivable   _____

Total Current Assets $_____

Long-Term Assets

Building $_____

Equipment   _____

Total Long-Term Assets $_____

Total Assets $_____

LIABILITIES & OWNER'S EQUITY

Current Liabilities

Bank Loans $_____

Other Loans (_____) _____

Accounts Payable _____

Sales Tax Payable _____

Total Current Liabilities $_____

Long-Term Liabilities

Mortgage Payable $_____

Total Long-Term Liabilities $_____

Total Liabilities $_____

Owner's/Shareholder's Equity $_____
_____, _____

Total Liabilities & Owner's Equity $_____

Use this portion of the Business Plan Project to complete a projected balance sheet for Section 3.5 ("Balance Sheet") of your business plan. Use Eva's business plan (on page 203 of the textbook) as a model.

Consider using a pie chart to show a same-size analysis of your income statement.

BUSINESS PLAN PROJECT 11.2

Name _____ Class _____ Date _____

Financial Ratios

Are my financial ratios good?

Return on Sales (ROS)

The formula for Return on Sales (ROS) is:

$$\text{(Net Profit} \div \text{Sales)} \times 100 = \text{Return on Sales (\%)}$$

1. Calculate your business's projected Return on Sales. Use the Net Profit and Sales from your Projected Annual Income Statement (on page 303 in Section 11.1 of this *Business Plan Project*).

   Projected First-Year Net Profit = $_____

   Projected First-Year Sales Revenue = $_____

   Return on Sales = _____%

Return on Investment (ROI)

The formula for Return on Investment (ROI) is:

$$\text{(Net Profit} \div \text{Initial Investment)} \times 100 = \text{Return on Investment (\%)}$$

2. Calculate your business's projected Return on Investment. Use the Net Profit from your Projected Annual Income Statement (on page 303 in Section 11.1 of this *Business Plan Project*). Use the Investment from your Projected Cash Flow Statement (on page 301 in Section 11.1 of this *Business Plan Project*).

   Projected First-Year Net Profit = $_____

   Projected Investment in First-Year Sales = $_____

   Return on Investment = _____%

Use this portion of the Business Plan Project to complete Section 3.6 ("Financial Ratios") of your business plan. Use Eva's business plan (on page 204 of the textbook) as a model.

Name _____ Class_____ Date _____

Break-Even Analysis

Break-Even Analysis

The break-even point is that moment when a business has sold exactly enough units to cover its expenses. Use break-even analysis to determine how many units of a product (or service) a business must sell to pay all its expenses.

The formula for determining your break-even units is:

Operating Expenses ÷ Contribution Margin = Break-Even Units

1. Calculate your business's projected Break-Even Units. Use the Fixed Operating Expenses from Section 10.1 (on page 295 of this *Business Plan Project*). Use the Contribution Margin per unit from Section 10.2 (on page 298 of this *Business Plan Project*).

   Projected First-Year Fixed Operating Expenses = $_____

   Projected First-Year Contribution Margin (per Unit) = $_____

   Break-Even Units = _____ Units

Break-Even Point

Now that you know the exact number of break-even units, you can determine the break-even point.

2. Refer to your first-two-years sales estimate from 9.2 (page 292 of this *Business Plan Project*). In what month (and which year, first or second) do you project that you will reach the number of units when you will break-even?

   _____

Use this portion of the Business Plan Project to complete Section 3.7 ("Break-Even Point") of your business plan. Use Eva's business plan (on page 204 of the textbook) as a model.

BUSINESS PLAN PROJECT
Section 13.1

Start-Up Investment

What types of financing are available?

Before you can start your business, you will need to analyze the start-up investment required. That's what this Section of the Business Plan Project will help you do. Then, if you are unable to finance the start-up investment yourself, you will need to determine how to obtain the necessary capital. That's what the next Section will help you with.

A start-up investment has two parts:

- *Start-up expenditures*
- *Cash reserves*

Start-Up Expenditures

Start-up expenditures are those expenses you will need to pay before you can start your business. Think of them as the things you need on the first day of business.

1. What are your start-up expenditures? In the following table, list the expenditures you need to start your business.

Start-Up Expenditures

Item	Cost
Total Start-Up Expenditures	

Cash Reserves

When starting a business, an entrepreneur needs to set aside extra money for two purposes: an Emergency Fund and a Reserve for Fixed Expenses.

2. Determine your emergency fund. *(This is the amount a business should have available in the first three to six months for emergencies.)* As a preliminary calculation, figure your emergency fund as one-half of your start-up expenditures.

   Start-Up Expenditures = $_____

   Emergency Fund (Start-Up Expenditures ÷ 2) = $_____

3. Determine your Reserve for Fixed Expenses. *(This is the amount required to cover your fixed operating expenses for 3 months.)* Use your estimated monthly fixed operating expenses from Section 10.1 (page 295 in this *Business Plan Project*).

   Estimated Monthly Fixed Operating Expense = $_____

   Reserve for Fixed Expenses (Estimated Monthly Fixed Operating Expenses × 3) = $_____

Start-Up Investment

4. Calculate your Start-Up Investment. Add your Start-Up Expenditures, your Emergency Fund, and your Reserve for Fixed Expenses.

Start-Up Investment

Start-Up Expenditures	$_____
Emergency Fund	$_____
Reserve for Fixed Expenses	$_____
Start-Up Investment	$_____

Use this portion of the Business Plan Project to begin to complete Section 3.8 ("Financing Strategy") of your business plan. (You'll add to it in the next Section of this Business Plan Project.) Use Eva's business plan (on page 204 of the textbook) as a model.

BUSINESS PLAN PROJECT 13.1

BUSINESS PLAN PROJECT
Section 13.2

Obtaining Financing

Should I obtain financing?

Deciding Whether to Finance

1. What is your start-up investment? (Use the amount from the previous Section.)

   $_____

2. How much of this start-up investment can you afford to pay yourself?

   $_____

3. How much of the start-up investment will you need to finance? (Subtract the amount you can afford to pay from the total start-up investment.)

   $_____

 ## Selecting Your Financing

4. If you need to finance some portion of your start-up investment, will you use debt financing?

   ☐ **Yes**   ☐ **No**

   If **Yes**, which form of debt financing will you use?

   ☐ Bank

   Write in the amount you hope to borrow. Then name the bank, with its address and telephone number.

   Borrowing: $_____

   _____

   _____

   _____

   _____

☐ Credit Union

Write in the amount you hope to borrow. Then name the credit union, with its address and telephone number:

Borrowing: $_____

_____

_____

_____

_____

☐ Relative or Friend

Write in the amount you hope to borrow. Then name the relative or friend, with his/her address and telephone number:

Borrowing: $_____

_____

_____

_____

_____

5. If you need to finance some portion of your start-up investment, will you use equity financing?

☐ **Yes**   ☐ **No**

If **Yes**, which form of equity financing will you use?

☐ Relative or Friend

Write in the amount you hope to obtain and the percentage of equity you will offer in exchange. Then name the relative or friend, with his/her address and telephone number.

Investment Sought: $_____

Equity Exchanged: _____

_____

_____

_____

_____

BUSINESS PLAN PROJECT 13.2

☐ Angels and Venture Capitalists

Write in the amount you hope to obtain and the percentage of equity you will offer in exchange. Then name the angel/venture capitalist, with his/her address and telephone number:

Investment Sought: $_____

Equity Exchanged: _____

_____

_____

_____

☐ Partner(s)

Write in the amount you hope to obtain and the percentage of equity you will offer in exchange. Then name the partner(s), with his/her/their address(es) and telephone number(s):

Investment Sought: $_____

Equity Exchanged: _____

_____

_____

_____

6. If you need to finance some portion of your start-up investment, will you use specialized sources of financing?

☐ **Yes**   ☐ **No**

If **Yes**, which form of specialized financing will you use?

☐ Small Business Investment Company (SBIC)

Write in the amount you hope to obtain and whether it will be debt or equity financing. (If equity financing, indicate the percentage of equity you will offer to exchange.) Then name the SBIC, with its address and telephone number.

Investment Sought: $_____

Equity Exchanged: _____

_____

_____

_____

☐ Minority Enterprise Small Business Investment Company (MESBIC)

Write in the amount you hope to obtain and whether it will be debt or equity financing. (If equity financing, indicate the percentage of equity you will offer to exchange.) Then name the MESBIC, with its address and telephone number.

Investment Sought: $_____

Equity Exchanged: _____

_____

_____

_____

☐ Customer Financing

Write in the amount you hope to obtain and whether it will be debt or equity financing. (If equity financing, indicate the percentage of equity you will offer to exchange.) Then name the customer, with his/her address and telephone number.

Investment Sought: $_____

Equity Exchanged: _____

_____

_____

_____

☐ Barter Financing

Write in the product or service you hope to obtain, and whether it will be debt or equity financing. (If equity financing, indicate the percentage of equity you will offer to exchange.) Then name the individual or company with whom you propose to barter, with the address and telephone number.

Barter for: _____

Offered in Exchange: _____

_____

_____

_____

Use this portion of the Business Plan Project to complete Section 3.8 ("Financing Strategy") of your business plan. (You started working on this in the last Section of this Business Plan Project.) Use Eva's business plan (on page 204 of the textbook) as a model.

BUSINESS PLAN PROJECT 13.2

BUSINESS PLAN PROJECT
Section 14.1

Recordkeeping

What records should I keep?

Types of Bank Accounts and Records

1. Indicate which type of bank accounts and records you will need as you start your business.

☐ Savings Account

☐ Checking Account

☐ Sales Receipts or Sales Invoices

☐ Purchase Orders

 ## Bank Accounts and Recordkeeping

2. Will you use a full- or part-time accountant (rather than doing the accounting yourself)?

☐ **Yes**   ☐ **No**

If **Yes**, who will you use? (Write his/her name, telephone number, and e-mail address).

_____

_____

_____

If **Yes**, how will the accountant or bookkeeper charge for his/her services?

_____

_____

_____

_____

Use this portion of the Business Plan Project to begin to complete Section 3.9 ("Recordkeeping & Accounting Systems") of your business plan. (You'll add to it in the next Section of this Business Plan Project.) Use Eva's business plan (on page 204 of the textbook) as a model.

Name _____ Class_____ Date _____

Accounting Systems

What kind of accounting system should I use?

Consider carefully the type of accounting system you are going to use. Once you start using a particular system, it may be hard to change to another one.

Accounting System

1. Which type of accounting system do you plan to use?

   ☐ Single-column approach

   ☐ Double-column approach

2. Do you plan to use a manual system or a computerized system?

   ☐ Manual *(Describe.)*

   _____

   _____

   _____

   _____

   _____

   ☐ Software/Computerized *(Describe.)*

   _____

   _____

   _____

   _____

   _____

Use this portion of the Business Plan Project to begin to complete Section 3.9 ("Recordkeeping & Accounting Systems") of your business plan. (You started working on this in the last Section of this Business Plan Project.) Use Eva's business plan (on page 204 of the textbook) as a model.

Executive Summary

Congratulations! You've completed the Standard Business Plan. In the process you've described in detail many aspects of your planned business. Now it's time to prepare an Executive Summary of the business plan as it now stands. Do this even if you are going on to complete the Advanced Business Plan. You'll discover that your perceptions can change as you work through the business-planning process.

Remember that an Executive Summary must be one page—no longer.

Mission Statement

3. What is your business's mission? Write your mission statement here in no more than two sentences. Refer to Section 4.1 of this *Business Plan Project* (page 251), if you need to.

_____

_____

_____

Business Name & Location

4. What is your business's name and where will it be located?

_____

_____

_____

Date Business Will Begin

5. When will your business formally begin operation?

_____

Owner's Name, Function, and Contact Information

6. What type of business ownership will be used? Refer to Section 3.2 of this *Business Plan Project* (page 247), if you need to. What are the roles and titles of the key people? Provide contact information for the important individuals in your business.

_____

_____

_____

_____

_____

BUSINESS PLAN PROJECT 14.2

Opportunity

7. Describe the opportunity as you see it. Refer to Section 6.2 of this *Business Plan Project* (pages 265–266), if you need to.

_____

_____

_____

_____

_____

_____

_____

Products or Services

8. Describe your business's products or services. Refer to Section 10.2 of this *Business Plan Project* (pages 297–298), if you need to.

One Unit of Sale = _____

Selling Price per Unit = _____

Contribution Margin per Unit = _____

Future Plans

9. Describe your plans for the future of your business. Refer to Section 8.1 of this *Business Plan Project* (pages 274-275), if you need to. Provide a brief mix of short-term, mid-range, and long-term goals.

_____

_____

_____

_____

_____

_____

_____

_____

Use this portion of the Business Plan Project to write an Executive Summary for your Standard Business Plan. Use Eva's business plan (on page 194 of the textbook) as a model.

BUSINESS PLAN PROJECT
Section 15.1

Hiring Decisions

What organizational structure is right for my business?

How should I staff my business?

How do I train and motivate employees?

Organizational Structure

1. What is your job title and role in your business?

_____

_____

_____

_____

_____

2. What type of organizational structure will you use when you begin your business? *Describe the structure and the various job titles. If you have someone in mind for a particular position, list that person's qualifications.*

_____

_____

_____

_____

_____

_____

_____

_____

_____

_____

BUSINESS PLAN PROJECT 15.1

3. Will your organizational structure change over the next five years as your business grows? *Describe how it will change and any new positions that might be created.*

_____

_____

_____

_____

_____

_____

_____

_____

_____

Use this portion of the Business Plan Project to begin to complete Section 4.1 ("Organizational Structures") of your business plan. Use Eva's business plan (on page 204 of the textbook) as a model.

Staffing

4. Will you be hiring outside professionals (such as lawyers, tax planners, consultants, accountants, etc.) in the next year?

☐ **Yes**   ☐ **No**

If **Yes**, describe the professionals you plan to hire. *Include the financial compensation you intend to provide.*

_____

_____

_____

_____

_____

_____

_____

_____

_____

Name _____ Class_____ Date _____

5. Based on your organizational needs, will you be hiring full- or part-time staff in the next year?

☐ **Yes**   ☐ **No**

If **Yes**, describe the positions:

Position: _____

Job Description: _____

_____

_____

Qualification: _____

_____

Compensation: $_____

Position: _____

Job Description: _____

_____

_____

Qualification: _____

_____

Compensation: $_____

Position: _____

Job Description: _____

_____

_____

Qualification: _____

_____

Compensation: $_____

Position: _____

Job Description: _____

_____

_____

Qualification: _____

_____

Compensation: $_____

Use this portion of the Business Plan Project to begin to complete Sections 4.2 ("Staffing") and 4.3 ("Outside Experts") of your business plan. Use Eva's business plan (on pages 204 and 205 of the textbook) as a model.

BUSINESS PLAN PROJECT 15.1

Name _____ Class_____ Date _____

Training & Motivating Employees

How do I train and motivate employees?

Employee Training

1. Do you have any personal plans for developing skills that will help you run your business? Will you be taking any courses, attending any workshops, going to any conferences or expos?

_____

_____

_____

_____

_____

_____

_____

2. If you have any employees, how do you plan to train them?

_____

_____

_____

_____

_____

_____

_____

_____

Motivating & Evaluating Employees

3. If you have employees, how do you plan to motivate them? *What would make an employee eager to work in your company? Will there be any performance-based rewards? Is job enlargement and job enrichment possible? How will you ensure that there is a positive work environment?*

_____

_____

_____

_____

_____

_____

_____

_____

4. If you have employees, when and how do you plan to evaluate them? Will promotion be possible?

_____

_____

_____

_____

_____

_____

_____

Use this portion of the Business Plan Project to begin to complete Section 4.4 ("Training and Motivating Employees") of your business plan. Use Eva's business plan (on page 205 of the textbook) as a model.

BUSINESS PLAN PROJECT 15.2

Name _____ Class _____ Date _____

Does my product involve intellectual property rights?
What contracts will my business require?

 Intellectual Property

1. Will your business involve copyrighting intellectual property?

   ☐ **Yes**   ☐ **No**

   If **Yes**, describe what intellectual property will need to be copyrighted.

   _____

   _____

   _____

   _____

   _____

   _____

   _____

2. Will your business involve patents?

   ☐ **Yes**   ☐ **No**

   If **Yes**, describe the product for which you intend to obtain a patent.

   _____

   _____

   _____

   _____

   _____

   _____

   _____

BUSINESS PLAN PROJECT 16.1

3. Do you intend to obtain a trademark or service mark for your business?

  ☐ **Yes**   ☐ **No**

  If **Yes**, describe your trademark or service mark. *(You can include a drawing of it, if you would like.)*

  _____

  _____

  _____

  _____

  _____

  _____

  _____

  _____

4. Does your business involve any trade secrets?

  ☐ **Yes**   ☐ **No**

  If **Yes**, describe how you intend to protect your company's trade secrets.

  _____

  _____

  _____

  _____

  _____

  _____

  _____

  _____

Use this portion of the Business Plan Project to begin to complete Section 5.1 ("Intellectual Property") of your business plan. Use Eva's business plan (on page 205 of the textbook) as a model.

Contracts

BUSINESS PLAN PROJECT 16.1

5. Will your business be a party to any of the following types of contracts?

☐ Lease

☐ Service Contract

☐ Sales Contract

☐ Confidentiality Agreement

☐ Nondisclosure Agreement

☐ Distribution Agreement

☐ Partnership Agreement

☐ Licensing Agreement

☐ Other type of contract (List _____)

6. For any of the above contracts you checked, fill in the following information.

Type of Contract: _____

Legal Advisor: _____

Key Points/Conditions: _____

_____

_____

Type of Contract: _____

Legal Advisor: _____

Key Points/Conditions: _____

_____

_____

Name _____ Class _____ Date _____

Type of Contract: _____

Legal Advisor: _____

Key Points/Conditions: _____

_____

_____

Type of Contract: _____

Legal Advisor: _____

Key Points/Conditions: _____

_____

_____

Type of Contract: _____

Legal Advisor: _____

Key Points/Conditions: _____

_____

_____

Type of Contract: _____

Legal Advisor: _____

Key Points/Conditions: _____

_____

_____

Use this portion of the Business Plan Project to begin to complete Section 5.2 ("Contracts") of your business plan. Use Eva's business plan (on page 205 of the textbook) as a model.

Name _____ Class _____ Date _____

How will I protect my business by using insurance?

 Insurance

1. Will your business require any of the following types of insurance?

   ☐ Property Insurance (including business interruption insurance)

   ☐ General Liability Insurance

   ☐ Product Liability Insurance

   ☐ Professional Liability Insurance

   ☐ Worker's Compensation Insurance

   ☐ Vehicle Insurance (Truck, Car, etc.)

   ☐ Other Type of Insurance (*Describe* _____)

2. For any of the above types of insurance that you checked, fill in the following information.

   Type of Insurance: _____

   Company: _____

   Agent: _____

   Coverage (Deductible, Payout, etc.): _____

   _____

   Annual Premium: $ _____

   Type of Insurance: _____

   Company: _____

   Agent: _____

   Coverage (Deductible, Payout, etc.): _____

   _____

   Annual Premium: $ _____

Name _____ Class_____ Date _____

Type of Insurance: _____

Company: _____

Agent: _____

Coverage (Deductible, Payout, etc.): _____

_____

Annual Premium: $ _____

Type of Insurance: _____

Company: _____

Agent: _____

Coverage (Deductible, Payout, etc.): _____

_____

Annual Premium: $ _____

Type of Insurance: _____

Company: _____

Agent: _____

Coverage (Deductible, Payout, etc.): _____

_____

Annual Premium: $ _____

Use this portion of the Business Plan Project to begin to complete Section 5.3 ("Insurance") of your business plan. Use Eva's business plan (on page 205 of the textbook) as a model.

BUSINESS PLAN PROJECT 16.2

BUSINESS PLAN PROJECT
Section 17.1

Taxes & Your Business

How will taxes affect my business?

Taxes

1. Will your business need to pay any of the following taxes?

   ☐ FICA (*Federal Insurance Contribution Act; Payroll Tax*)

   ☐ State Income Tax *(Payroll Tax)*

   ☐ Federal Unemployment Tax

   ☐ Sales Tax

   ☐ Corporate Income Tax (Only for Corporations)

   ☐ Property Tax

   ☐ City Tax

   ☐ Other Tax (*Describe* _____)

2. For any of the above taxes that you checked, fill in the following information.

Type of Tax: _____
Estimated Annual Payment: $_____
Payments Due: _____
Form Used (if any): _____

Type of Tax: _____
Estimated Annual Payment: $_____
Payments Due: _____
Form Used (if any): _____

Name _____ Class _____ Date _____

Type of Tax: _____

Estimated Annual Payment: $_____

Payments Due: _____

Form Used (if any): _____

Type of Tax: _____

Estimated Annual Payment: $_____

Payments Due: _____

Form Used (if any): _____

Type of Tax: _____

Estimated Annual Payment: $_____

Payments Due: _____

Form Used (if any): _____

Type of Tax: _____

Estimated Annual Payment: $_____

Payments Due: _____

Form Used (if any): _____

Use this portion of the Business Plan Project to begin to complete Section 5.4 ("Taxes") of your business plan. Use Eva's business plan (on page 205 of the textbook) as a model.

BUSINESS PLAN PROJECT 17.1

BUSINESS PLAN PROJECT
Section 17.2

Government Regulations

How will government regulations affect employees?

Government Regulations

1. What kinds of government regulations related to employee-protection and workplace safety will affect your business?

   ☐ Fair Labor Standards Act *(establishes minimum hourly wage, minimum age, overtime, and maximum hours worked)*

   ☐ Occupational Safety and Health Administration (OSHA) Regulations *(focuses on safety in the workplace)*

   ☐ Anti-Discrimination regulations *(outlaws discrimination based on age, gender, religion, race, ethnicity, disabilities, or marital status)*

   ☐ Other Employee-Protection or Workplace Regulations
   (Describe _____ *)*

2. What kinds of government regulations related to customer issues will affect your business?

   ☐ Labeling Regulations *(such as the Fair Packaging and Labeling Act, and the Food, Drug, and Cosmetics Act)*

   ☐ Product Safety Regulations *(often set by the U.S. Consumer Product Safety Commission, CPSC)*

   ☐ Other Regulations Related to Customer Issues
   (Describe _____ *)*

3. What kinds of government regulations related to competition and advertising will affect your business?

   ☐ Truth-in-Advertising Regulations *(established by the Federal Trade Commission, FTC, such as the Fair Packaging and Labeling Act, and the Food, Drug, and Cosmetics Act)*

   ☐ Price Fixing or Price Discrimination Regulations

   ☐ Other Regulations Related to Competition and Advertising
   (Describe _____ *)*

BUSINESS PLAN PROJECT 17.2

4. Will you need any licenses or permits for your business?

☐ **Yes**   ☐ **No**

If **Yes**, describe the license and/or permits you will need for your business.

_____

_____

_____

_____

_____

_____

_____

_____

_____

_____

5. Will you need to comply with any zoning laws or other laws related to a property, commercial use, building appearance, parking lot, or signage?

☐ **Yes**   ☐ **No**

If **Yes**, describe the requirements of the laws.

_____

_____

_____

_____

_____

_____

_____

_____

_____

BUSINESS PLAN PROJECT 17.2

6. Will you need to comply with any environmental protection regulations?

□ **Yes**   □ **No**

If **Yes**, describe the requirements of the laws.

_____

_____

_____

_____

_____

_____

_____

_____

_____

_____

_____

Use this portion of the Business Plan Project to begin to complete Section 5.5 ("Government Regulations") of your business plan. Use Eva's business plan (on page 205 of the textbook) as a model.

Name _____ Class_____ Date _____

How will I manage my business?

Leadership Skills

1. The success or failure of a business, especially a new business, depends on the leadership skills of the entrepreneur. Leaders are responsible for the effectiveness of organizations, both large and small. They provide a vision and influence the activities of individuals and groups within the organization.

   Take the following leadership survey to evaluate your leadership characteristics. ("1" represents low; "10" represents high).

Leadership Skill	Explanation	Range									
Rapport	Getting along well with others	1	2	3	4	5	6	7	8	9	10
Human relations	Communicating well and believing in teamwork	1	2	3	4	5	6	7	8	9	10
Passion	Being motivated and dedicated to excellence	1	2	3	4	5	6	7	8	9	10
Perseverance	Sticking to task or goal; keeping things on track and moving forward	1	2	3	4	5	6	7	8	9	10
Risk-taking	Not being afraid to take chances	1	2	3	4	5	6	7	8	9	10
Responsibility	Being accountable for actions	1	2	3	4	5	6	7	8	9	10
Open-mindedness	Willing to consider new things	1	2	3	4	5	6	7	8	9	10
Able to delegate	Assigning the right people to the right tasks	1	2	3	4	5	6	7	8	9	10
Enthusiasm	Being energetic and positive	1	2	3	4	5	6	7	8	9	10
Able to organize	Having life and work in order	1	2	3	4	5	6	7	8	9	10
Decisiveness	Being comfortable making decisions	1	2	3	4	5	6	7	8	9	10
Wisdom	Showing intelligence and competence	1	2	3	4	5	6	7	8	9	10
Persuasiveness	Being able to convince and influence others	1	2	3	4	5	6	7	8	9	10
Honesty	Being open and truthful	1	2	3	4	5	6	7	8	9	10

Name _____ Class _____ Date _____

Integrity	Being fair and gaining the trust of others	1	2	3	4	5	6	7	8	9	10
Competitiveness	Being eager to win	1	2	3	4	5	6	7	8	9	10
Flexibility	Coping with new situations	1	2	3	4	5	6	7	8	9	10
Understanding	Showing empathy and respecting the needs of others	1	2	3	4	5	6	7	8	9	10
Discipline	Being focused and strong	1	2	3	4	5	6	7	8	9	10
Vision	Being able to see the "big picture" and focus on goals	1	2	3	4	5	6	7	8	9	10
Influence	Motivating and inspiring people to cooperate and pursue goals	1	2	3	4	5	6	7	8	9	10
Handles pressure	Being able to handle frustration and pressure	1	2	3	4	5	6	7	8	9	10
Empowerment	Empowering others to make decisions; sharing praise and credit	1	2	3	4	5	6	7	8	9	10
Handles conflict	Having a healthy approach to conflict and disagreement	1	2	3	4	5	6	7	8	9	10
Coaching ability	Teaching, assisting, and answering questions	1	2	3	4	5	6	7	8	9	10
TOTAL SCORE _____											

Company Image

2. What kinds of company image would you like for your business? Describe the perception that you would want the public to have of your company.

_____

_____

_____

_____

_____

_____

This portion of the Business Plan Project is for your own use in thinking about your company. It doesn't appear in the Business Plan Template.

Name _____ Class_____ Date _____

Managing Expenses, Credit, & Cash Flow

How do I manage expenses, credit, and cash flow?

 ## Trade Credit

1. Will your business need to establish trade credit with another business? *Describe the types of companies with which you will need to establish trade credit.*

_____

_____

_____

_____

_____

2. Will you extend trade credit to other businesses? Describe the types of companies to which you will extend trade credit.

_____

_____

_____

_____

_____

 ## Consumer Credit

3. Will you offer consumers credit? Will you allow credit cards? Will you provide other types of consumer credit or extended payment plans? *Describe your plans for consumer credit.*

_____

_____

_____

_____

Projected Monthly Cash Flow

4. What will your average monthly cash flow look like in your first year? *Fill in the following form.*

CASH INFLOWS

Cash Sales	$_____
Total Cash Inflows	$_____

CASH OUTFLOWS

Variable Expenses: Materials	$_____
Variable Expenses: Labor	_____
Other Variable Expenses (_____)	_____
Advertising	_____
Insurance	_____
Interest	_____
Telephone	_____
Utilities (Gas, Electric)	_____
Other Fixed Expenses (_____)	_____
Other Fixed Expenses (_____)	_____
Other Fixed Expenses (_____)	_____
Other Fixed Expenses (_____)	_____
Total Cash Outflows	$_____

CASH AVAILABLE $_____

Here's how to fill in this form:

- "Cash Sales": Divide your annual sales estimate by 12. (*Your annual sales estimate is from Section 9.2, page 292, of this Business Plan Project. This, however, assumes that all your sales are cash, not credit.*)

- Variable Expenses: Divide your projected annual variable expenses by 12. (*Your projected annual variable expenses are from Section 11.1, page 303*).

- Fixed Expenses: Divide your projected annual fixed expenses by 12. (*Your projected annual fixed expenses are from Section 11.1, page 303*).

- "Cash Available": Subtract the Total Cash Outflows from the Total Cash Inflows.

Use this portion of the Business Plan Project to begin to complete Section 6.1 ("Expenses, Credit, and Cash Flow") of your business plan. Use Eva's business plan (on page 206 of the textbook) as a model.

Name _____ Class _____ Date _____

BUSINESS PLAN PROJECT
Section 19.1

Managing Production & Distribution

How do I manage production and distribution?

  Site Selection & Layout Planning

1. Where will you locate your business? (*If you don't yet have a location, then describe the type of site you will be looking for. Include the price you are willing to pay for rent, etc.*)

   _____

   _____

   _____

   _____

   _____

   _____

   _____

   _____

2. How will you layout your business space? Will you have layout considerations at your business site?

   _____

   _____

   _____

   _____

   _____

   _____

   _____

   _____

Production Management

3. How will you maintain high productivity at your business?

_____

_____

_____

_____

_____

_____

_____

4. Will any part of your business be automated?

☐ **Yes**   ☐ **No**

If **Yes**, describe how it will be automated? Also describe how you will maintain the equipment you will be using.

_____

_____

_____

_____

_____

_____

_____

5. How will you maintain quality in your product or service?

_____

_____

_____

_____

_____

Name _____ Class_____ Date _____

6. Construct a Gantt chart to show the schedule for opening your business. *(See page 514 of the textbook for an example. You can use a time frame of months.)*

Gantt Chart: Schedule for Starting the Business

Task	Month 1	Month 2	Month 3	Month 4	Month 5	Month 6
1.						
2.						
3.						
4.						
5.						
6.						
7.						
8.						
9.						
10.						
11.						
12.						
13.						
14.						
15.						

Distribution Management

7. Will your business involve a distribution chain (distribution channels)? How will you maintain high productivity at your business?

☐ **Yes**   ☐ **No**

If **Yes**, show the distribution chain. *(Include the markup and price at each level. Use actual company names whenever possible.)*

Manufacturer: _____

Product Price: $_____

Intermediary: _____

Markup: _____%

Product Price: $_____

Intermediary: _____

Markup: _____%

Product Price: $_____

Retailer: _____

Markup: _____%

Product Price: $_____

8. Will your business involve shipping or transporting products to other businesses or consumers?

☐ **Yes**   ☐ **No**

If **Yes**, describe how your products will be shipped. *Also indicate the cost of shipping and the delivery terms.*

_____

_____

_____

_____

_____

9. Will your business be receiving incoming goods?

☐ **Yes**   ☐ **No**

If **Yes**, describe how you will handle incoming goods.

_____

_____

_____

_____

_____

10. Will your business involve storage or warehousing?

☐ **Yes**   ☐ **No**

If **Yes**, describe how store your materials or goods.

_____

_____

_____

_____

_____

_____

_____

Use this portion of the Business Plan Project to begin to complete Section 6.2 ("Production and Distribution") of your business plan. Use Eva's business plan (on page 206 of the textbook) as a model.

Consider including the Gantt Chart in your business plan.

Name _____ Class_____ Date _____

Managing Operations

How do I manage my operations?

 Business Policies

1. What are my business's hours of operation?

_____

_____

_____

2. What is the business's policy regarding extending credit to customers? *You will need to have a clear statement describing the conditions required for customers to buy from you on credit. See page 522 of the textbook for a description of the Three C's: Character, Capacity, and Capital.*

_____

_____

_____

_____

_____

_____

3. What is the business's policy regarding returns and rework requests? How will your company handle customer complaints? *You will need to establish policies for handling situations when products are returned by dissatisfied customers or when customers are not happy with the service your company provided.*

_____

_____

_____

_____

_____

_____

4. Does your business require shipping or delivery to your customers?

☐ **Yes**   ☐ **No**

If **Yes**, what is your business's policy regarding shipping/deliveries? *These are guidelines that your customers will need to know about shipping/delivery options, cost, and estimated length of time before they receive the products.*

_____

_____

_____

_____

_____

_____

5. Will your company have a warranty?

☐ **Yes**   ☐ **No**

If **Yes**, describe the warranty.

_____

_____

_____

_____

_____

_____

6. Are there any other issues related to customer service that should be included in your business plan?

☐ **Yes**   ☐ **No**

If **Yes**, what are they?

_____

_____

_____

_____

Use this portion of the Business Plan Project to begin to complete Section 6.3 ("Operations") of your business plan. Use Eva's business plan (on page 206 of the textbook) as a model.

BUSINESS PLAN PROJECT 19.2

BUSINESS PLAN PROJECT
Section 20.1

Managing Purchasing

How do I manage purchasing?

Managing Purchasing

1. Is purchasing important for my business?

   ☐ **Yes**   ☐ **No**

   If Yes, continue with this section of the Business Plan Project.

2. How will I select the right quality? *Consider using some type of value analysis (a process for assessing the performance of a product or service relative to its cost).*

   _____

   _____

   _____

   _____

   _____

   _____

3. How will I select the right quantity? *Make sure to base your purchasing decisions on your projected sales estimates in Section 10.2, page 292, in this Business Plan Project.*

   _____

   _____

   _____

   _____

   _____

   _____

4. How will I purchase at the right time? *Will you use periodic reordering or nonperiodic reordering? What is the lead time required for purchasing?*

_____

_____

_____

_____

_____

_____

_____

5. How will I choose the right vendors? *What are the factors to consider in choosing a vendor? Fill out the following chart to show vendors being considered.*

Vendor Analysis

Factor	Vendor A	Vendor B	Vendor C
1.			
2.			
3.			
4.			
5.			
6.			
7.			

6. How will I get the right price? *Will you be able to take advantage of quantity discounts or trade discounts?*

_____

_____

_____

_____

_____

_____

_____

7. How will I get the right payment terms? *What payment terms would you prefer? Will it be possible to get those terms?*

_____

_____

_____

_____

_____

_____

_____

_____

Use this portion of the Business Plan Project to begin to complete Section 6.4 ("Purchasing") of your business plan. Use Eva's business plan (on page 207 of the textbook) as a model.

BUSINESS PLAN PROJECT
Section 20.2

Managing Inventory

How do I manage inventory?

 Managing Inventory

1. Is managing inventory important for my business?

   ☐ **Yes**   ☐ **No**

   If Yes, continue with this section of the Business Plan Project.

2. What will my inventory level be when I start the business? *How many units do you plan to have on hand on the first day of business?*

   _____

   _____

   _____

3. What will the value of the inventory be when you start the business? *Multiply the expense of the product by the number of units on hand on your first day.*

   $_____

4. How much do you estimate you will spend on inventory in your first year?

   $_____

5. How many times during your first year do you think you will buy inventory? *This is referred to as your Investment Purchase in the formula in step #6.*

   _____

6. What is your average annual inventory investment? The formula for the average annual inventory turnover is:

   Total Inventory Investment ÷ Number of Investment Purchases

   The average annual inventory investment is $_____

BUSINESS PLAN PROJECT 20.2

Name _____ Class _____ Date _____

7. What is your inventory turnover? The formula for the inventory turnover is:

Total Inventory Investment ÷ Average Annual Inventory Investment

The inventory turnover is _____

8. What type of inventory system will you use?

☐ Visual Inventory System

☐ Perpetual Inventory System

☐ Periodic Inventory System

☐ Partial Inventory System

☐ Just-In-Time Inventory System

Use this portion of the Business Plan Project to begin to complete Section 6.5 ("Inventory") of your business plan. Use Eva's business plan (on page 207 of the textbook) as a model.

Name _____ Class _____ Date _____

Planning for Business Growth

How can I plan for business growth?

Short-Term Business Goals

1. What are your short-term business goals? *Describe your goals for the business in the next year.*

_____

_____

_____

_____

_____

_____

_____

_____

_____

_____

_____

Long-Term Business Goals

2. What strategy will you use for long-term growth?

☐ Intensive Growth Strategy *(emphasizes market penetration, market development, or product development)*

☐ Integrative Growth Strategy *(emphasizes acquisitions and mergers; vertical integration or horizontal integration)*

☐ Diversification Growth Strategies *(emphasizes new products or services that are different from the core business; synergistic diversification or horizontal diversification)*

3. What are your long-term business goals? *Describe your goals for the business over the next three to five years and beyond.*

_____

_____

_____

_____

_____

_____

_____

_____

_____

_____

_____

_____

_____

Use this portion of the Business Plan Project to begin to complete Section 7.1 ("Business Growth") of your business plan. Use Eva's business plan (on page 207 of the textbook) as a model.

BUSINESS PLAN PROJECT
Section 21.2

Challenges of Growth

What are the challenges of growth?

Personal Feelings about Growth

Answer the following questions based on the assumption that your business is successful.

1. How do you imagine spending your time on an average day?

_____

_____

_____

_____

_____

_____

2. How much do you realistically expect to earn from your business in a year?

$_____

3. What are your personal goals for the next five years? What do you hope to accomplish?

_____

_____

_____

_____

_____

_____

_____

_____

4. Write a one-sentence "vision statement" for your business that describes what you would like to achieve over the next five years.

_____

_____

_____

_____

_____

_____

Short-Term Business Challenges

5. What are your short-term business challenges? *What kind of things could happen in the next year that would limit your chances of growth?*

_____

_____

_____

_____

_____

_____

_____

_____

_____

_____

_____

_____

BUSINESS PLAN PROJECT 21.2

Long-Term Business Challenges

6. Which of the following areas could pose a challenge to your business's long-term growth?

☐ Physical Space *(outgrow the room, office, building)*

☐ Business Structure *(need to change the organizational structure)*

☐ Materials and Equipment *(need to purchase more materials or equipment)*

☐ Information Technology *(need new computers, software, etc.)*

☐ People and Skills *(need more employees, new skills)*

☐ Money *(need financing)*

7. Based on the previous question, describe in detail the challenges to your business's long-term growth.

_____

_____

_____

_____

_____

_____

_____

_____

_____

_____

_____

_____

Use this portion of the Business Plan Project to begin to complete Section 7.2 ("Challenges") of your business plan. Use Eva's business plan (on page 207 of the textbook) as a model.

Name _____ Class _____ Date _____

Franchising & Licensing

Can I franchise or license my business?

Franchising Your Business

1. Do you plan eventually to franchise your business?

   ☐ **Yes** ☐ **No**

   If **Yes**, describe why you think your business can be franchised.

   _____

   _____

   _____

   _____

   _____

Licensing a Brand

2. Do you plan eventually to license a brand that you have developed?

   ☐ **Yes** ☐ **No**

   If **Yes**, describe why you think your brand can be licensed.

   _____

   _____

   _____

   _____

   _____

Use this portion of the Business Plan Project to begin to complete Section 7.3 ("Franchising and Licensing") of your business plan. Use Eva's business plan (on page 207 of the textbook) as a model.

Name _____ Class_____ Date _____

When and how should I leave my business?

 Exit Strategy

1. When might you decide to leave your business? *Base your answer on your personal considerations, the condition of the business, and the condition of the economy.*

   _____

   _____

   _____

2. When you leave the business, what would you estimate its net sales revenue would be? *Base this partially on your sales estimates from Section 9.2 of this Business Plan Project (pages 292–294) and partially on your plan for growing the business in Section 22.1 (page 356).*

   $_____

3. Use the following formula to place a value on your business at the time you plan to leave it. *(You will use a multiplier of 3.)*

   Net Sales Revenue × 3 = Value of Business

   The value of your business at the time you plan to leave would be $_____.

4. At the time you exit your business, will it have goodwill that adds additional value?

   ☐ **Yes**   ☐ **No**

   If **Yes**, describe what type of goodwill you believe the business will have.

   _____

   _____

   _____

   _____

5. Describe how you will exit your business. *(Some possibilities are: sale of the business, management buyout, employee stock ownership plan, and an initial public offering.)*

_____

_____

_____

_____

_____

_____

_____

_____

_____

6. Will you have investors in you business at the time you plan to exit it?

☐ **Yes**   ☐ **No**

If **Yes**, describe how your exit strategy will appeal to them.

_____

_____

_____

_____

_____

_____

_____

_____

_____

Use this portion of the Business Plan Project to begin to complete Section 7.4 ("Exit Strategy") of your business plan. Use Eva's business plan (on page 207 of the textbook) as a model.

Take the time to review your entire business plan, including your Executive Summary. As you develop a business plan, you may discover new aspects of your business. Make sure your business plan is consistent and represents your most current thoughts.

BUSINESS PLAN PROJECT 22.2

Personal Goals and Building Wealth

An important aspect of starting and running a business is to realize your personal goals and to build your personal wealth. The following questions focus on those concerns.

7. Describe your financial goals:

   a. One year from now

   _____

   _____

   _____

   _____

   _____

   b. Five years from now

   _____

   _____

   _____

   _____

   _____

   c. Ten years from now

   _____

   _____

   _____

   _____

   _____

   d. Twenty years from now

   _____

   _____

   _____

   _____

   _____

BUSINESS PLAN PROJECT 22.2

8. Describe your risk tolerance. What are some of the factors that affect your risk tolerance?

_____

_____

_____

_____

9. Think of an item you would like to buy. Answer the following questions to develop a plan for saving the money to buy it.

    a. How much does the item cost? $_____

    b. How much money do you make each week? $_____

    c. If you put 10% of that money aside, how much would you be saving weekly? $_____

    d. How long would it take to save enough money to buy the item? _____

10. What percent of your net income do you plan to save to achieve your personal financial goals?

_____%

11. How much will you need to make a down payment on a home?

You will need a down payment to secure a mortgage, which is a loan from a bank to purchase a home. The down payment is often 10% of the price. For example, with a down payment of $15,000, you could probably buy a $150,000 home.

Down payment = $_____

12. How many years do you have to save for your first home?

_____ years

13. Based on Questions 11 and 12, fill in the following statement:

"I plan to save a down payment of $_____ so that I can buy my first home at age _____ for $_____."

14. What do you plan as a career?

_____

_____

_____

_____

15. What is the annual salary for the type of career for which you are planning?

    $ _____

16. Based on Questions 14 and 15, fill in the following statement:

    "I plan to work toward a career as a _____ with a
    starting annual salary of $ _____."

17. Do you know how much education you will need for your chosen career?

    ☐ **Yes**   ☐ **No**

    If **Yes**, describe the education you will need for your chosen career.

    _____

    _____

    _____

    If **No**, how do you plan to find out what education you will need for your chosen career?
    (Possibilities include: research online or asking a teacher, parent, or mentor).

    _____

    _____

    _____

18. Do you know how much money it will take for you to achieve the education you desire?

    ☐ **Yes**   ☐ **No**

    If **Yes**, indicate how much money you will need to achieve the education you desire.
    (Indicate what the money will be used for.)

    _____

    _____

    _____

    If **No**, how do you plan to find out how much money you will need to achieve the education
    you will need for your chosen career? *(Possibilities again include: research online or asking a
    teacher, parent, or mentor).*

    _____

    _____

    _____

BUSINESS PLAN PROJECT 22.2

19. Do you know of any scholarship opportunities you could apply for?

☐ **Yes**   ☐ **No**

If **Yes**, describe the scholarship opportunities you would be eligible to apply for. *(Make sure to indicate the deadline for applying.)*

_____

_____

_____

_____

_____

If **No**, how do you plan to find out about scholarship opportunities? *(Possibilities include: research online, resources in the school library, or asking a teacher, parent, or mentor).*

_____

_____

_____

_____

_____

Business Plan Template

Fill in sections of the Business Plan Template as you complete the appropriate sections of the *Business Plan Project*. The Business Plan Template is also available as a word-processing document on the Student Center at *entrepreneurship.pearson.com*.

If you need more space to write a section of your business plan, use the additional blank business plan pages at the end of the Business Plan Template. Make sure to indicate the business plan section and section title on the blank business plan page.

Name _____ Class _____ Date _____

BUSINESS PLAN

Name of Business: _____

Motto: _____

EXECUTIVE SUMMARY

Mission Statement

_____

_____

Business Name & Location

_____

_____

Date Business Will Begin

_____

Owner's Name, Function, & Contact Information

_____

_____

_____

Contact Information: _____

_____

Opportunity

_____

_____

_____

_____

Product (or Service)

_____

_____

_____

Economics of One Unit

One Unit of Sale = _____

Selling Price per Unit = $ _____

Contribution Margin per Unit = $_____

Future Plans

_____

_____

BUSINESS PLAN

Name of Business: _____

Motto: _____

1. BUSINESS IDEA

1.1 Qualifications

_____
_____
_____
_____
_____
_____
_____
_____
_____
_____

1.2 Factors Influencing Demand

_____
_____
_____
_____
_____
_____
_____
_____
_____
_____
_____

1.3 Type of Business

_____
_____
_____
_____

BUSINESS PLAN TEMPLATE

1.5   Social Responsibility

_____

_____

_____

_____

_____

_____

_____

_____

_____

_____

_____

_____

2.   OPPORTUNITY & MARKET ANALYSIS
2.1   Business Opportunity

_____

_____

_____

_____

_____

_____

_____

_____

_____

_____

_____

_____

_____

_____

2.2   Market Research

_____

_____

_____

_____

_____

_____

_____

_____

_____

_____

_____

_____

2.3   Competitors

Direct Competition: _____

_____

_____

_____

_____

_____

_____

_____

Indirect Competition: _____

_____

_____

_____

_____

_____

_____

_____

2.4　Competitive Advantage

_____

_____

_____

_____

_____

_____

_____

_____

_____

_____

_____

2.5　Marketing Plan

_____

_____

_____

_____

_____

_____

_____

_____

_____

_____

_____

_____

_____

_____

_____

_____

_____

_____

BUSINESS PLAN TEMPLATE

2.6 Pricing Strategy

_____

_____

_____

_____

_____

_____

2.7 Promotion

_____

_____

_____

_____

_____

_____

_____

_____

_____

_____

_____

_____

_____

_____

2.8 Sales Methods

_____

_____

_____

_____

_____

_____

Name _____ Class _____ Date _____

3. FINANCIAL STRATEGIES
3.1 Sales Estimates: Years 1 and 2

_____

_____

_____

_____

_____

_____

_____

_____

_____

_____

	Year 1		Year 2	
Month	Units	Sales Revenue	Units	Sales Revenue
January				
February				
March				
April				
May				
June				
July				
August				
September				
October				
November				
December				
Annual Totals				

Name _____ Class _____ Date _____

3.1 Sales Estimates: Years 3 and 4

_____

_____

_____

_____

_____

_____

_____

_____

_____

_____

Month	Year 3		Year 4	
	Units	Sales Revenue	Units	Sales Revenue
January				
February				
March				
April				
May				
June				
July				
August				
September				
October				
November				
December				
Annual Totals				

3.1   Sales Estimates: Year 5 and Beyond

_____

_____

_____

_____

_____

_____

_____

_____

_____

_____

	Year 5	
Month	Units	Sales Revenue
January		
February		
March		
April		
May		
June		
July		
August		
September		
October		
November		
December		
Annual Totals		

Name _____Class_____Date _____

3.2   Business Expenses

_____

_____

_____

Operating expenses for the first year of business will be:

- Advertising: $_____
- Depreciation: $_____
- Insurance, Auto: $_____
- Insurance, Health: $_____
- Insurance, Life: $_____
- Interest: $_____
- Rent: $_____
- Salaries: $_____
- Telephone: $_____
- Utilities: $_____
- Other: $_____

3.3   Economics of One Unit

ONE UNIT OF SALE = _____

SELLING PRICE (PER UNIT): $_____

  Variable Costs

    Cost of Goods Sold

      Materials $_____

      Labor ($ _____ per Hour)   _____

      Cost of Goods Sold $_____

    Other Variable Costs

      Commissions $_____

      Shipping & Handling   _____

      Other Variable Costs   _____

    Total Variable Costs   _____

CONTRIBUTION MARGIN (PER UNIT): $_____

3.4 Income Statement

PROJECTED ANNUAL INCOME STATEMENT
MONTHLY INCOME STATEMENT
End of First Year

REVENUE

Sales $\qquad$ $_____

Total Revenue $_____

COST OF _____ SOLD

Labor _____ $_____

Materials _____ _____

Cost of _____ Sold _____

GROSS PROFIT $_____

OPERATING EXPENSES

Advertising $_____

Depreciation _____

Insurance _____

Interest _____

Telephone _____

Rent _____

Salaries _____

Utilities (Gas, Electric) _____

Other Fixed Costs (_____) _____

Total Operating Expenses _____

PRE-TAX PROFIT $_____

Taxes (_____%) _____

NET PROFIT $_____

3.5 Balance Sheet

PROJECTED ANNUAL BALANCE SHEET
End of First Year

ASSETS

Current Assets

Cash $_____

Inventory   _____

Accounts Receivable   _____

Total Current Assets $_____

Long-Term Assets

Building $_____

Equipment   _____

Total Long-Term Assets $_____

Total Assets $_____

LIABILITIES & OWNER'S EQUITY

Current Liabilities

Bank Loans $_____

Other Loans (_____)   _____

Accounts Payable   _____

Sales Tax Payable   _____

Total Current Liabilities $_____

Long-Term Liabilities

Mortgage Payable $_____

Total Long-Term Liabilities $_____

Total Liabilities $_____

Owner's/Shareholder's Equity $_____

_____, _____

Total Liabilities & Owner's Equity $_____

BUSINESS PLAN TEMPLATE

3.6 Financial Ratios

Return on Sales (ROS): _____

_____

_____

_____

Return on Investment (ROI): _____

_____

_____

_____

3.7 Break-Even Point

_____

_____

_____

_____

_____

_____

_____

3.8 Financing Strategy

Start-Up Investment: _____

_____

_____

_____

Reserve for Fixed Investments: _____

_____

_____

_____

Start-Up Expenditures & Emergency Fund: _____

_____

_____

_____

3.9 Recordkeeping & Accounting Systems

_____

_____

_____

4. ORGANIZATIONAL STRUCTURES

4.1 Organizational Structure

_____

_____

_____

_____

_____

_____

_____

_____

_____

_____

4.2 Staffing

_____

_____

_____

_____

_____

4.3 Outside Experts

_____

_____

_____

4.4   Training and Motivating Employees

_____

_____

_____

_____

_____

_____

5.   LEGAL STRUCTURES

5.1   Intellectual Property

_____

_____

_____

_____

_____

_____

5.2   Contracts

_____

_____

_____

_____

_____

5.3   Insurance

_____

_____

_____

_____

_____

_____

5.4   Taxes

_____

_____

_____

_____

_____

_____

5.5   Government Regulations

_____

_____

_____

_____

_____

_____

6.   BUSINESS MANAGEMENT
6.1   Expenses, Credit, and Cash Flow

_____

_____

_____

_____

_____

_____

_____

_____

_____

MONTHLY CASH FLOW BUDGET

CASH INFLOWS

Cash Sales $_____

Total Cash Inflows $_____

CASH OUTFLOWS

Variable Expenses: Materials $_____

Variable Expenses: Labor   _____

Other Variable Expenses (_____)   _____

Advertising   _____

Insurance   _____

Interest   _____

Rent   _____

Salaries   _____

Telephone   _____

Utilities (Gas, Electric)   _____

Other Fixed Expenses (_____)   _____

Total Cash Outflows $_____

CASH AVAILABLE $_____

6.2 Production and Distribution

_____

_____

_____

_____

_____

_____

_____

_____

_____

BUSINESS PLAN TEMPLATE

6.3   Operations

Hours of Operation: _____

_____

_____

_____

Returns/Rework Requests: _____

_____

_____

_____

Client Satisfaction: _____

_____

_____

_____

6.4   Purchasing

_____

_____

_____

_____

_____

_____

6.5   Inventory

_____

_____

_____

_____

_____

_____

_____

7.   PLAN FOR GROWTH

7.1   Business Growth

Short-Term Business Goals: _____

_____

_____

_____

_____

_____

_____

Long-Term Business Goals: _____

_____

_____

_____

_____

_____

_____

_____

7.2   Challenges

Short-Term Business Challenges: _____

_____

_____

_____

_____

Long-Term Business Challenges: _____

_____

_____

_____

_____

_____

BUSINESS PLAN TEMPLATE

7.3   Franchising and Licensing

_____

_____

_____

_____

_____

_____

_____

_____

7.4   Exit Strategy

_____

_____

_____

_____

_____

_____

_____

_____

_____

_____

_____

_____

_____

_____

_____

_____

BUSINESS PLAN TEMPLATE

Name _____ Class _____ Date _____

Section: _____

_____

_____

_____

_____

_____

_____

_____

_____

_____

_____

_____

_____

_____

_____

_____

_____

_____

_____

_____

_____

_____

_____

_____

_____

_____

_____

_____

BUSINESS PLAN TEMPLATE

Name _____ Class _____ Date _____

Section: _____

_____
_____
_____
_____
_____
_____
_____
_____
_____
_____
_____
_____
_____
_____
_____
_____
_____
_____
_____
_____
_____
_____
_____
_____
_____
_____

BUSINESS PLAN TEMPLATE

Name _____ Class _____ Date _____

Section: _____

_____

_____

_____

_____

_____

_____

_____

_____

_____

_____

_____

_____

_____

_____

_____

_____

_____

_____

_____

_____

_____

_____

_____

_____

_____

_____

_____

_____

BUSINESS PLAN TEMPLATE

Name _____ Class _____ Date _____

Section: _____

_____

_____

_____

_____

_____

_____

_____

_____

_____

_____

_____

_____

_____

_____

_____

_____

_____

_____

_____

_____

_____

_____

_____

_____

Name _____ Class_____ Date _____

Section: _____

Name _____ Class _____ Date _____

Section: _____

Name _____ Class _____ Date _____

Section: _____

_____

_____

_____

_____

_____

BUSINESS PLAN TEMPLATE

Name _____ Class _____ Date _____

Section: _____